Cocktails
Across America

Cocktails

ACROSS

America

A Postcard View of Cocktail Culture in the 1930s, '40s, and '50s

BY DIANE LAPIS & ANNE PECK–DAVIS

Foreword by Douglass Miller

The Countryman Press
A division of W. W. Norton & Company
Independent Publishers Since 1923

Page 42, photograph of Landy R. Hales poster by Don Dement.
Page 166, postcard of San Trancisco Trolley Car by Stanley Piltz,
© Wagener-Erganian Collection.
Page 168, Curt Teich postcard from The Newberry, Chicago's
Independent Research Library, Chicago, Illinois.

For information about permission to reproduce selections from this
book, write to Permissions, The Countryman Press, 500 Fifth Avenue,
New York, NY 10110

For information about special discounts for bulk purchases,
please contact W. W. Norton Special Sales at
specialsales@wwnorton.com or 800-233-4830

Manufacturing through Imago
Book design by Paul Nielsen, Faceout Studio
Production manager: Devon Zahn

The Countryman Press
www.countrymanpress.com

A division of W. W. Norton & Company, Inc.
500 Fifth Avenue, New York, NY 10110
www.wwnorton.com

978-1-68268-144-2

10 9 8 7 6 5 4 3 2 1

*We dedicate this book to
our loving husbands,*

*Clifford L. Davis
and
Peter Lapis*

CONTENTS

FOREWORD

Cocktails Across America takes the reader on a journey to the drinking establishments famous in the 1930s, 1940s, and 1950s. The book brings to life cocktail bars from generations ago, many of which no longer exist. The authors, Diane Lapis and Anne Peck-Davis, have selected postcards that show where some of the greatest cocktails were created. Paired with previously untold narratives and fascinating trivia, you can look at the postcards, recreate the cocktail from the recipes provided, and experience another time in American history.

Today, it is easy to record a vacation or evening out. At the push of a button or a tap of a screen, you can take numerous photos and video. Years ago, however, you had to physically exchange the photo or slide with an individual in order to share the experience. It was often simpler to purchase a postcard and mail it to family and friends. Postcards, therefore, became a valuable record of the decor and ambience of post-Prohibition drinking and eating establishments.

Linen postcards appeared in the early 1930s and remained in production during the post-Prohibition years. The cards had a slight texture that allowed the ink color to pop and be more vibrant. Linen postcards allowed people to see faraway places more clearly and in more vivid color than could earlier postcards and photographs.

When Diane and Anne first showed me their collection, I was transported to a culture long gone. They have a massive collection of linen postcards on a wide range of subjects, from everyday muses to hotels, bars, and tourist destinations. It is magical to experience the midcentury restaurant and drinking culture through the gorgeous postcards of the era.

A personal favorite of mine is a postcard of the Carousel Bar at the Hotel Monteleone in New Orleans. I have attended the International Cocktail Convention, Tales of the Cocktail, which is held at the Hotel Monteleone. The event brings out today's industry leaders in the cocktail world. The heart of the conference is centered at the Carousel Bar.

The bar was designed to look and revolve like a carousel, a theme that was popular in the post-Prohibition years and that appeared in bars all over the country. Today, the Carousel Bar is the only current example of this type of bar design. The linen postcards featured in this book permit us to see how different bars, restaurants, hotels, and travel looked in the past. *Cocktails Across America* provides the reader with a unique opportunity to experience the post-Prohibition, World War II, and post-war years through interesting stories, period imagery, and vintage recipes.

Cheers,

Douglass Miller
Certified Wine and Spirits Specialist

INTRODUCTION

Drinks on the house! On December 5, 1933, revelers legally imbibed once more as the 21st Amendment became fully ratified, ending the nationwide prohibition on alcohol. Americans were delighted that the "Great Experiment" was over, though times remained tough as they struggled through the Great Depression and World War II. Many sought solace and entertainment in movie theaters, watching Fred Astaire and Ginger Rogers dance, sing, and drink the night away in chic clubs. Atmospheric restaurants and cocktail lounges began to emerge, mimicking the more glamorous life on the silver screen. Guests were offered an opportunity to escape the humdrum of their daily activities.

After Prohibition, drinking establishments proliferated. Many of these venues were advertised on linen postcards. Produced between 1931 and the late 1950s, these bright, colorful postcards portrayed the fun and joy that could be found at a particular hotel, restaurant, or supper club. Printed on a patterned card stock that resembled linen, airbrushed images in rainbow hues and utopian ambience turned the ordinary into the spectacular. New cocktails were created during this period and old ones were served again. Some were forgotten entirely and revived years later. Tastes changed and new ingredients crept into the American market, including rum, tequila, and vodka, influencing post-Prohibition cocktails.

As Americans developed a taste for the exotic, many whimsical bars and restaurants opened to meet the demand. It was possible to receive a linen postcard from a friend depicting a circus-, zoo-, or aquatic-themed establishment, or one with European, Asian, or Latin motifs. Don the Beachcomber's Polynesian-themed establishment set off a trend of tropical-inspired drinks and venues later known as tiki bars. Trader Vic's provided a way to enjoy an exotic environment while choosing from many newly popular rum-based drinks, such as the Mai Tai. It is easy to imagine sipping a carefully constructed concoction while dreaming of tropical breezes in a faraway place. Elegant Art Deco clubs treated guests to streamlined, futuristic decor where they could listen to jazz or dance to a big band. Drinks were served with a flourish, reviving vintage cocktails or adding new twists to old favorites. When viewing the interiors of these lavish venues, one can easily imagine the fun and optimism guests experienced as they toasted to a bright tomorrow.

Advancements in mechanical capabilities and techniques found a creative use in establishments during the 1930s, 1940s, and 1950s. Some hotels and lounges installed a "merry-go-round" revolving bar, allowing thrilled patrons the novelty of taking a spin while enjoying their favorite drink. Ice-skating shows were also part of the supper club scene, stemming from the popularity of Olympic skating star Sonja Henie and her appearance in Hollywood films. The ability to freeze small stages with ice started a popular trend referred to as "tank shows." What could be more entertaining than eating, drinking, and watching ice-skating performances on indoor ice rinks? Technological breakthroughs in bowling, including the use of automatic pin-setters, bolstered the popularity of this sport and—in no time—bowling alley clubs popped up, offering guests a drink between frames.

The travel industry changed rapidly after Prohibition. Americans were able to travel on high-speed trains, planes, and ships. Each form of transportation provided opportunities to imbibe, whether in elegant lounges, dining cars, or plane cabins. The immense popularity of train travel in grand streamlined locomotives meant guests could drink to their destinations in Art Deco style. Some trains were so famous they had cocktails named in their honor. The air industry introduced in-flight cocktails midcentury. Ships, outfitted with bars and dance halls, were already a big draw for tourists, precursors to the modern "booze cruises."

Linen postcards provide a unique portal into what nightlife was like in the post-Prohibition, World War II, and post-war years. To enhance this experience, we have paired the vintage cocktail recipes with stories about the people, places, and locations depicted in the images. Through period vignettes, colorful postcards, and inventive recipes, prepare to be transported to another time and place in American history, drinks in hand!

BLUE MIRROR — 824 FOURTEENTH STREET, N. W. — WASHINGTON, D. C.   SB-H1058

Hickory House

MIAMI BEACH, FLA.

144 WEST 52nd STREET
NEW YORK

23rd and Liberty Ave., just around the corner, Miami Beach, Florida

Service with Charm!

THE SHERATON-BILTMORE HOTEL
Providence, Rhode Island

East Coast

3A-H59

20th Century Cocktail

Roll out the red carpet! The *20th Century Limited* is here! This cocktail was created in honor of New York Central Railroad's luxury express train that ran between New York's Grand Central Terminal and Chicago's LaSalle Street Station from 1902 to 1967, touted as the "most famous train in the world." Surprisingly, the cocktail was not created in America, but actually appeared in *The Café Royal Cocktail Book*, a publication compiled by the president of the United Kingdom's Bartender's Guild in 1937. A brilliant combination of ingredients, including gin, Lillet Blanc, white crème de cacao, and fresh lemon juice, make this cocktail as smooth and intriguing as the train itself.

In 1936, industrial designer Henry Dreyfuss successfully completed a project for New York Central Railroad, winning him the opportunity to redesign its most famous train, the

20th Century Limited . Working in collaboration with the Pullman Company and New York Central engineers, Dreyfuss created a streamlined version of the train that became an icon for the era. Making its initial run from New York to Chicago in a record-breaking 16 hours on June 15, 1938, a red carpet was literally rolled out welcoming upscale passengers to the train's brand-new Art Deco environment. Dreyfuss designed everything from the Cyclops eye spotlight on the locomotive to the interior and exterior of the passenger cars. The coaches were decorated in Machine-Age tones of gray and blue with rust-colored highlights.

Passengers were treated to plush leather seating, installed in the train's public spaces, creating a country club atmosphere. Dreyfuss left nothing to chance, designing streamlined dinnerware, coordinating uniforms, and bedclothes. Strength, hope, and invincibility personified the image of this train as society propelled through the twentieth century on the eve of World War II. An appropriate tribute to this powerful, iconic train, the 20th Century Cocktail is crisp and cool with just the right hint of luxury.

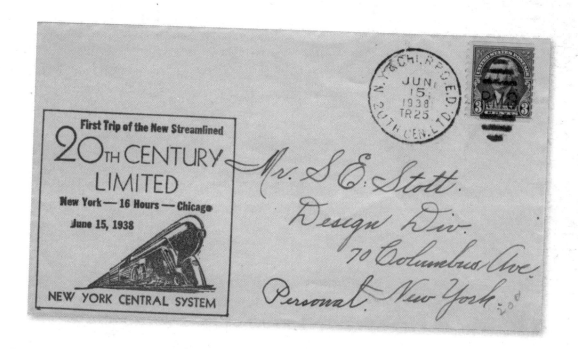

20th Century Cocktail

2 ounces gin
1 ounce Lillet Blanc
¾ ounce white crème de cacao
1 ounce fresh lemon juice
Lemon twist, for garnish

Place all ingredients in a cocktail shaker filled with ice. Shake until moisture forms on the outside of the container. Pour into a chilled glass and garnish with a lemon twist.

INTERIOR, GRAND CENTRAL STATION NEW YORK CITY

Dempsey Cocktail

On a blistering hot Fourth of July in 1919, Jess Willard, the defending heavyweight-boxing champion, stepped into the ring with a scrappy kid from Colorado named Jack Dempsey. The odds were against Dempsey, who came in 60 pounds lighter and 6 inches shorter than the towering Willard. Dempsey was a hungry fellow who honed his boxing skills in saloon fights and street brawls. By the end of the first round, Dempsey had knocked Willard down an astonishing seven times. At the start of the fourth round, Willard was so bloodied his corner threw in the towel. Dempsey, nicknamed the "Manassa Mauler," became the new heavyweight champion and the fight remains steeped in controversy to this day.

How did Dempsey inflict such damage on the huge Willard? Were his gloves loaded? Would the fight have gone differently had the bell not malfunctioned at the beginning of the first round? These are questions that have been debated for years.

JACK DEMPSEY'S RESTAURANT, 50th St. at 8th Ave. Opp. Madison Square Garden, New York City

But one thing is sure—Dempsey became an American hero.

After retiring from boxing, Dempsey went into the restaurant business. By 1938, he opened Jack Dempsey's Broadway Restaurant, best remembered for its location between 49th and 50th Street in New York City. The gregarious Dempsey was often found at the bar, greeting guests, signing autographs, and posing for pictures. Dempsey set out to create a restaurant that was "a gathering place for sportsmen, fight men, journalists, and celebrities." He met his goal with great success and the restaurant remained open for decades.

Customers visiting Dempsey's bar were impressed by James Montgomery Flagg's 18-foot mural of the landmark Dempsey-Willard fight. In the mural, nationally renowned sportswriters sit ringside: Damon Runyon, Grantland Rice, Ring Lardner, and Rube Goldberg. Rice declared Dempsey to be one of the finest men he met in his sportswriting career. Dempsey returned the favor stating, "I was a pretty good boxer, but the writers made me great." When the restaurant closed,

Dempsey donated the painting to the National Portrait Gallery at the Smithsonian Institution, where it presently hangs.

The Dempsey Cocktail appears in Robert Vermeire's book, *Cocktails: How to Mix Them* (1922), and was created to commemorate Dempsey's 1921 title defense against Georges Carpentier. The cocktail packs a wallop. One round is all you need!

 # Dempsey Cocktail

1 ounce gin
1 ounce Calvados
2 dashes absinthe
2 dashes grenadine

Shake all ingredients in a cocktail shaker filled with ice and strain into a chilled cocktail glass.

"*The Meeting Place of the World*"
Jack Dempsey's Broadway Restaurant

Red Snapper

The Red Snapper, also known as the Bloody Mary, made its debut at the St. Regis Hotel in New York City. Fernand Petiot, formerly of Harry's New York Bar in Paris, introduced this spicy combination of vodka and tomato juice when he took his post as head barman at the St. Regis' King Cole Bar and Lounge in 1934. The King Cole Bar was named in honor of the 25-foot-long mural of Old King Cole painted by Maxfield Parrish and installed in 1932 at the St. Regis Hotel.

Supremely wealthy, John Jacob Astor IV built the St. Regis Hotel on 5th Avenue and 55th Street before his untimely death aboard the Titanic. Opening in 1904, the hotel was the pinnacle of luxury at the peak of the Gilded Age. Caroline Astor personally set the standard of operation and the hotel has a long history of catering to the crème de la crème of society. The Old King Cole mural was commissioned by John Jacob Astor IV for his Knickerbocker Hotel and created by Parrish in

1906. From the Knickerbocker Hotel it was placed in storage before finding its present home at the St. Regis' King Cole Bar.

From 1938 until 1947, the hotel operated the Iridium Room, a swanky supper club adjacent to the King Cole Bar. The Iridium Room was an elegant venue, hosting well-choreographed ice-skating shows accompanied by a live orchestra. Imagine the thrill diners experienced when a small ice-skating rink emerged from beneath the orchestra and over the dance floor. The shows featured popular professional skaters of the time such as Dorothy Lewis and Carol Lynne. Following the show, the rink would retract beneath the orchestra and guests could dance the night away.

The winning combination of Petiot's Red Snapper and Parrish's mural have presided over the King Cole Bar, serving an amazing array of notable guests including Salvatore Dali and his ocelot, Marlene Dietrich, and Babe Paley.

 # Red Snapper

2 ounces tomato juice
2 ounces vodka
½ teaspoon Worcestershire Sauce
1 pinch salt
1 pinch cayenne pepper
1 dash fresh lemon juice

Shake all ingredients in a cocktail shaker with ice and serve in a tall glass.

La Guardia Field, New York, N. Y.

Aviation Cocktail

The Aviation Cocktail is a lovely drink to behold. The crème de violette, a liqueur with violet flower flavoring and hue, turns a sky blue when mixed with gin and lemon juice.

Hugo Ensslin, the head bartender at the Hotel Wallick in New York City, included the Aviation Cocktail in his 1916 compilation *Recipes for Mixed Drinks*. It was one of the last cocktail books published before the beginning of Prohibition. The Hotel Wallick, and its adjacent neighbor the Hotel Claridge, would not survive the devastating monetary effects of Prohibition. Although the owners were following the letter of the law and not serving alcohol, patrons were going to other establishments in the neighborhood to enjoy their cocktails illegally. The Wallick changed hands as well as its name. It became the Cadillac Hotel and eventually closed in 1939.

The Wright Brothers' 1903 flight marked the beginning of air travel. Perhaps the Aviation Cocktail was so named to

Hotel New Yorker Aviation Terrace   LaGuardia Field

capitalize on the public's sudden interest in manned flight, or simply because of its periwinkle color. Air travel and its namesake drink were quite a sensation during its infancy. A local paper from Rochester, New York, stated that, "the aviation cocktail is the latest. But, after all, aren't all cocktails of the aviation variety?" In the 1920s, only wealthy passengers could afford to travel to places such as Nassau and Havana, enabling partygoers a fashionable way to drink legally during Prohibition.

TIMES SQUARE AT NIGHT, NEW YORK CITY

5A-H648

CADILLAC RESTAURANT BAR AND GRILL—1500 BROADWAY.

BETWEEN 43RD AND 44TH STREETS, NEW YORK CITY.

It wasn't until the introduction of the DC-3 in the 1930s that air travel became affordable for the masses. The plane's speed, reliability, passenger comfort, and ability to operate from short runways made continental and transcontinental flights possible for the first time. Air travel was so trendy that flight themes took over restaurants. The Hotel New Yorker Aviation Terrace at LaGuardia Airport in New York provided a quick respite for passengers to enjoy a meal before their flight. A 1940s Aviation Terrace menu included cocktails such as the Kitty Hawk, Airways Special, the Airport Punch, and the Non-Skid (a non-alcoholic concoction).

When boarding a flight, travelers were handed postcard images of their plane or in-flight meal. A positive pitch to friends and family back home was a vital aspect of marketing for the airlines. The Aviation Cocktail is a classic that reflects the nation's excitement in the nascent days of air travel.

☞ Aviation Cocktail

2 ounces gin
1 ounce fresh lemon juice
½ ounce Maraschino liqueur
¼ ounce crème de violette
Cherry, for garnish

Shake all the ingredients in a cocktail shaker with ice. Strain into a cocktail glass. Garnish with a cherry.

THE LOUNGE RESTAURANT

Cugat Triple C Cocktail

It is a summer evening. A taxi pulls into the Park Avenue entrance of the Waldorf Astoria Hotel in New York City. A two-some exits the cab and climbs hand-in-hand seventeen steps to the grand lobby of the famed hotel. The happy couple takes an elevator to the Starlight Roof where they will dine and dance to the exotic rhythms of Xavier Cugat and His Orchestra.

Cugat was celebrated as the "Rhumba King" for introducing Latin American rhythms to American dance halls, moviegoers, and radio listeners. As a teenager, Cugat played the violin and accompanied Italian tenor Enrico Caruso during his tours to America. Caruso was an amateur caricaturist and taught the eager Cugat how to draw. When Cugat realized that he would never be a musical virtuoso, he applied his artistic talents as a political cartoonist at the *Los Angeles Times*. Cugat returned to the music scene after a two-year stint at the newspaper. In the 1920s, he formed a band that performed in short films and at the Cocoanut Grove in Hollywood.

Cugat led the Waldorf Astoria Orchestra from 1933 to 1949, presenting music and dance styles that combined the big band sound with Latin rhythms. His distinctive arrangements blended the waltz and fox trot with the rhumba, mambo, samba, bolero, and tango. Enthusiastic diners enjoyed fantastical floorshows and those inclined to dance swayed to the beat of South American musicians dressed in native costume. Audiences were introduced to exotic instruments such as the claves, marimba, maracas, and bongo. Cugat would often lead the orchestra with his violin bow while holding a Chihuahua dog. In 1935, he introduced the conga at the Waldorf, where dancers formed a long serpentine line, shuffled three steps, and kicked slightly ahead of the fourth step. Cugat's congas were considered the "Big Town's biggest thrills."

THE WALDORF-ASTORIA. THE "UNOFFICIAL PALACE OF NEW YORK" NEW YORK CITY 40

Cugat drew caricatures throughout his career; his quick study and caustic wit captured the likes of musicians, dancers, actors, and politicians. Newspapers featured his cartoons of the rich and famous, from Broadway to Hollywood. More than 70 larger-than-life-size caricatures adorned the Lounge Restaurant at the Waldorf during his tenure there. Inset colored fluorescents surrounded the dance floor, adding to the room's ambience. In addition to his conducting, musical arrangements, and drawings, Cugat recorded hundreds of songs and appeared as himself in film and radio programs. In newspaper interviews, Cugat revealed that he enjoyed baseball, bullfights, roast beef, and the Triple C, the "Cugat Conga Cocktail," a drink named after the dance he popularized.

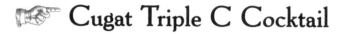 Cugat Triple C Cocktail

2 ounces white rum
½ ounce grenadine
¾ ounce fresh lime juice
1 dash absinthe

Shake all ingredients in a cocktail shaker with ice and strain into cocktail glass.

CARICATURES BY
XAVIER CUGAT

LOUNGE RESTAURANT *The* WALDORF-ASTORIA
NEW YORK

Zombie Cocktail

What do the 1939–40 New York World's Fair, famous jazz musician Fats Waller, and an impresario named Monte Proser have in common? The Zombie Cocktail! This potent, Tiki-style drink was created by Don Beach for his bar in Hollywood, California. Upon his return from French Polynesia, he opened his Don the Beachcomber establishment, incorporating elements of the tropics in the decor, as well as plenty of rum-based drinks. It was here that the Zombie was created in the 1930s and Beach carefully guarded his recipe by coding the bottles of ingredients.

The success of Beach's bar did not go without notice and it was not long before competing entrepreneurs emulated the Tiki style. One such person was New York-based entrepreneur Monte Proser. With links to organized crime, Proser was a creative force in the nightclub and entertainment business.

55W   Trylon and Perisphere, New York World's Fair

© N. Y. W. F.

BA-H955

Not one to miss a business opportunity, Proser promoted the Zombie drink as "Monte Proser's Zombie" on the midway at the 1939–40 New York World's Fair.

Wedged between the Great Depression and World War II, the 1939–40 New York World's Fair offered visitors a magnificent extravaganza and an optimistic view for a hopeful future. Dotting the fairgrounds were great streamlined buildings filled with technological showcases, information, and entertainment. The amusements included showman Billy Rose's Aquacade. With a stage set 60 feet out on Fountain Lake, guests could watch beautiful showgirls, colorful water displays, and synchronized swimming.

The Aquacade is mentioned in Fats Waller's 1940 recording of "Abercrombie Had a Zombie." The song is a true testament to the potency of the Zombie drink. In the song, Abercrombie, a meek and law-abiding citizen, has a few Zombies and winds up wading into the Aquacade, among other shenanigans.

A combination of four kinds of rum and fruit juices, the Zombie was invented on the West Coast but gained true notoriety on the East Coast. Proser, Waller, and the famous New York World's Fair were influential in making this drink part of the American landscape. Always on the move, Proser went on to conceptualize the Copacabana Nightclub in New York and was referred to as "The Genius" by Frank Sinatra.

WATER STADIUM AT NIGHT. NEW YORK WORLD'S FAIR OF 1939

 # Zombie Cocktail

Juice of one lime
½ ounce pineapple juice
½ ounce papaya juice
1 teaspoon brown sugar
1½ ounces golden rum
1 ounce dark rum
½ ounce white rum
Splash of 151-proof rum

Stir juices and brown sugar into a cocktail shaker. Add ice and all rum except the 151-proof rum. Shake and strain into an ice-filled glass. Float the 151-proof rum on top.

Popular Dance Orchestras

A Gala Private Party

"Where Every Party is a Banquet"
FRANK PALUMBO'S CABARET-RESTAURANT
Famous for Food Since 1884   PHILADELPHIA, PA.
824-830 Catherine Street

Floor Shows Nightly

Private Room for Banquets in an Atmosphere of Friendly Hospitality

MAIN DINING ROOM — SEATS 800 PERSONS

Cabaret Cocktail

Cabaret nightclubs and restaurants were popular destinations for fun-seekers after Prohibition ended. Patrons could dine and drink while being entertained by music, dancing, and other amusements. While American cabaret was influenced by European and Latin American productions, entrepreneurs put their own stamp on the style and substance in their venues. Cabaret venues often employed a master of ceremonies who sometimes acted as bandleader and entertainer.

The Tropicana Nightclub in Havana, Cuba was considered to be the largest and most beautiful cabaret and casino in the world. Opened in 1939, it featured Afro-Cuban music with a chorus line of 50 dancers in flashy sequin-and-feather-adorned costumes. Two New York City clubs, the Copacabana and the Latin Quarter, fashioned their venues after the Tropicana with beautifully outfitted chorines, vaudeville acts, and big names in show business

MONTE PROSER'S
COPACABANA
NEW YORK
MINIMUM CHARGE
(Per Person)
Weekdays & Sundays - $3.00
Sat., Hol. & Hol. Eves - $4.00

CHICAGO'S BEAUTIFUL THEATRE RESTAURANT
Latin Quarter
THEATRE RESTAURANT
23 WEST RANDOLPH STREET

COCKTAIL CIRCLE

MAIN DINING ROOM

such as Mae West, Frank Sinatra, and Jimmy Durante. Carmen Miranda was one of the most famous performers at the Tropicana, the Copacabana, and the Latin Quarter. She was a Brazilian film star and talented nightclub singer and dancer, known for her signature fruit-studded turban and exotic clothes. The Copa, originally called the Villa Vallée, featured master of ceremonies Rudy Vallée, a singer, bandleader, actor, and entertainer.

Music from nightclubs, restaurants, and hotels were broadcast on the radio. Movies and television shows brought the music, dance, and culture of cabaret into households across America. In the sitcom, *The Lucy-Desi Comedy Hour*, Lucy meets her future husband Ricky Ricardo while on vacation in Cuba. She arranges for Ricky to audition in Rudy Vallée's orchestra, allowing him to immigrate to America. Soon after, he is employed as a bandleader at the fictitious Tropicana Club in New York.

Frank Palumbo's Cabaret Restaurant in Philadelphia,

Pennsylvania, led a variety of unusual acts to entertain guests that included acrobats, jugglers, trick drummers, and the wild and hilarious antics of Pluto the Wonder Horse. Popular crooners and dance combos encouraged patrons to dance after dinner. The Cabaret Cocktail celebrates the glitzy and glamorous cabarets in post-Prohibition America.

Cabaret Cocktail

1 ounce gin
3/4 ounce Lillet Blanc or Capertif
1/4 ounce Bénédictine
1 dash absinthe
1 dash Angostura bitters
Cherry, for garnish

Stir with ice and strain into a cocktail glass. Garnish with a cherry.

Diamondback Cocktail

The Lord Baltimore Hotel, centrally located in the heart of Baltimore, Maryland, was the go-to place for sophisticated travelers, high society, and debutantes. The hotel, built in 1928, is a splendid example of French Renaissance style and features an exquisite two-story lobby crowned by gilded, coffered ceilings. The elegant ballroom is noted for its brass fixtures, tall columns, and Baccarat crystal chandeliers. A recently discovered speakeasy was located in a corner behind the restaurant. The hotel is now listed on the National Register of Historic Places.

The Diamondback Cocktail was created in the hotel's 100-seat Diamondback Lounge located in the lower lobby, although the date of origin is not known. Ted Saucier first cited the namesake drink, the Diamondback, in his cocktail book, *Bottoms Up* (1951).

Lord Baltimore Hotel

Hanover and Baltimore Streets, Baltimore, Md.

3A-H191

Most cocktail enthusiasts associate this drink with the diamondback snake due to the drink's alcoholic "bite." However, the creator of the Diamondback was probably referencing the diamondback terrapin or turtle, native to the Chesapeake Bay area. From the beginning of the twentieth century, terrapin soup—prepared with broth, cream, terrapin meat, and rye—was popular in the more exclusive restaurants, hotels, private clubs, and elite households.

Landy R. Hales, a Baltimore-born artist and inventor, created the Diamondback Lounge's bold advertising poster and menu depicting a well-dressed turtle sporting a top hat, bowtie, and cane. Its shell, naturally, is encrusted with diamonds. In 1956, patrons would have enjoyed perusing the Lounge's eight-page menu filled with over sixty cocktails, 113 different spirits, and fifteen beers. The turtle reference brings this drink home to its roots in Maryland.

Diamondback Cocktail

1½ ounces rye whiskey
¾ ounce Applejack
¾ ounce Yellow Chartreuse

Shake all ingredients in a cocktail shaker with ice until cold. Strain over ice in a rocks glass.

Du Pont Hotel Cocktail

The Renaissance-style Hotel du Pont opened to great fanfare in 1913. Pierre S. du Pont was president of the DuPont Company, one of the largest chemical companies in the world. He conceived the idea to give the city of Wilmington, Delaware, the most beautiful hotel in the country. During the first week of operation, 25,000 people streamed into the building to view this no-expense-spared hostelry. Guests could dine in the elegant Green Room, lodge in one of 300 guest rooms and enjoy the theater all under one roof. A palatial 1,220-seat theater called the Playhouse was built within the walls of the hotel. The theater's construction was considered to be a remarkable technical feat of its day. The hall showcased Broadway's dress rehearsals and local performances.

72637

Nylon Suite, Hotel du Pont, Wilmington, Delaware

118:—THE DUPONT CHEMISTRY BUILDING.

For decades, the Hotel du Pont's Grill Room was the social heart for Delawareans. It featured a long bar, welcoming fireplace, and wainscoting and pillars decorated with beer-drinking and card-playing gnome carvings. After dining in the exclusive Green Room, patrons would walk down the rose marble staircase to the Grill Room, enjoy a cocktail and dance to five-star orchestras and bands. During Prohibition, the Grill Room served only lunch, but a well-known bootlegger delivered whiskey to hotel guests hidden in men's and ladies' clothing boxes with the logos of Wilmington's finest shops. Mr. du Pont, although a conservative drinker, did not agree with Prohibition and worked toward its repeal. He helped draft liquor laws for Delaware as the chairman of the Delaware State Alcoholic Beverage Commission.

The Hotel du Pont's guest rooms featured nylon upholstery, curtains, and rugs. It was DuPont that developed and introduced this synthetic fiber to epic crowds at the 1939–40 New York World's Fair. Live models "Miss Chemistry" and "Miss

Nylon" wore and demonstrated nylon stockings as an inexpensive alternative to wearing silk. Consumer production halted during World War II as DuPont manufactured nylon exclusively for war materials. As soon as the war ended, nylon riots ensued throughout the nation with women lining up by the thousands to purchase a limited supply of hosiery. The use of nylon fabrics in blouses, scarves, gloves, dresses, and hats made fashionable clothing affordable to the mass-market.

The Grill Room was bursting with 400 celebrants on New Year's Eve in 1947. Dinner and dancing returned to the hotel after a long hiatus due to the war. Women donned evening gowns and were seen on the arms of soldiers in dress uniforms. A toast to the end of the war and a sip of the Du Pont Hotel cocktail was a perfect way to welcome in a hopeful 1948.

Du Pont Hotel Cocktail

1¼ ounces brandy
1 ounce dry sherry
1 dash Angostura bitters
Orange twist, for garnish

Stir with ice and strain into cocktail glass. Serve with a twist of orange peel.

A Steel Mill at the Steel Center of the World, Pittsburgh, Pa. — D-14

Duquesne Club Whiskey Sour

It was December 10, 1934, opening day of the newly remodeled ladies' dining room at the Duquesne Club in Pittsburgh, Pennsylvania. In hopes of attracting the cocktail-gowned crowd, the Club created a rendezvous for women to imbibe cocktails in-between manicures, luncheons, and guild meetings. A gleaming white crescent-shaped cocktail bar and a lounge decorated in pastel blues, grays, silver, and gold lent a note of merriment and modernity to an otherwise masculine room.

Prohibition had been repealed for a year, and women across the nation were beginning to drink in public. Three hundred club-members' wives filled the room to overflowing, sharing in conversation, whiskey sours, and martinis. There was, however, some consternation about this form of "impropriety." When members saw photographs the following day in the newspapers of women drinking at the private club, there was an outcry!

The Duquesne Club was founded in 1873 as a private men's club. Business titans discussed modernizations, mergers, and marketing while enjoying billiards, cigars, fine meals, and good whiskey. The earliest members were prominent industrialists and entrepreneurs of steel, oil, railroad, and banking such as Andrew Carnegie, Henry Clay Frick, Henry Heinz, and Andrew Mellon. The brownstone boasted eleven magnificent dining rooms and twenty private luncheon rooms serving more than 600 guests daily, a veritable "who's who" in Pittsburgh.

Joseph Pandl began his career at the Duquesne Club as a busboy in 1923. He later studied to be a headwaiter under Oskar at the Waldorf Astoria and eventually became the maître d'hôtel at the Duquesne Club in 1927. After World War II, Pandl enlisted the aid of club members to help restore his devastated hometown in Heiligenkreuz, Austria, by securing clothing,

medicine, and supplies. Pandl received a Distinguished Service Medal from the Austrian government and became the first honorary member of the Duquesne Club. While managing the demanding operations of the Club, Pandl created recipes such as the "Lobster a la Joe" and potato chips served in the Viennese fashion, by curiously piling them in folded napkins. Three of Pandl's cocktail recipes appeared in Saucier's 1951 *Bottoms Up* cocktail book: Before Lunch, Morning After, and the Duquesne Club Whiskey Sour featured here.

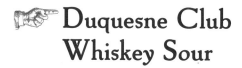 # Duquesne Club Whiskey Sour

1 egg white
2 ounces rye whiskey
Juice of ½ lemon
1 teaspoon granulated sugar

Place the egg white in the cocktail shaker and dry shake vigorously until the egg white becomes frothy. Add ice and all other ingredients in the shaker and continue to shake vigorously. This may take a few minutes. Strain into a highball glass filled with ice.

SKYLINE OF BUSINESS SECTION FROM GRANDVIEW PARK AT NIGHT, PITTSBURGH, PA.

THE CAVALIER HOTEL, VIRGINIA BEACH, VA

16

61687

Cavalier Cocktail

In the 1930s, Virginia Beach became a destination for the rich and famous. The Cavalier Hotel was the grandest hotel to cater to well-heeled guests. Overlooking the Atlantic Ocean, the striking brick building opened in 1927. A private depot was constructed to accommodate guests traveling nonstop from Chicago to the Cavalier via the Norfolk and Western Railroad. In 1929, the Cavalier Beach Club was added to complete this playground for society's elite.

Limousines arrived at the front door of the Cavalier, where guests could enjoy the healthful benefits of a saltwater bath available in each room. Shops in the lower lobby included a hair salon, clothing store, and ice cream parlor. A medical doctor was available at the hotel, and a stockbroker's office contained a ticker tape direct from the New York Stock Exchange.

On America's East Coast, there was no other place that booked more headlining entertainers, jazz musicians, swing

bands, and big-name personalities. Musicians such as Benny Goodman, Cab Calloway, Glenn Miller, Les Brown, and Harry James performed to a guest list that included Bette Davis, Judy Garland, and Will Rogers. Dancing and dining were available at the Beach Club in the afternoon and under the stars each night.

The Cavalier Cocktail mirrors the aristocratic atmosphere in which it was created. A combination of Bénédictine, brandy, and lime juice, topped with champagne offered a potent, refreshing, and luxurious combination to guests, celebrants, and partygoers. The Cavalier Cocktail is a representation of the glamorous evenings, top entertainment, and elegant service guests experienced at this seaside resort.

147:—DANCING AT THE WATER'S EDGE, CAVALIER BEACH CLUB, VIRGINIA BEACH, VA.

48906

 Cavalier Cocktail

½ ounce Bénédictine
1 ounce brandy
Juice of 1 lime
4 ounces champagne

Place Bénédictine, brandy, and lime juice in a cocktail
shaker with ice. Shake and strain into a champagne glass.
Top with champagne.

PB-107 *Royal Palm Way*
PALM BEACH, FLORIDA

Palm Beach Special

A symbol of sun-drenched luxury, the Palm Beach Special is a reflection of resort living and glamorous afternoons at the pool. Warm breezes, a turquoise ocean, and palm trees swaying above one's lounge chair are the inspiration for this appealing drink. Presented in *Charles' Book of Punches and Cocktails* (1934), this sunset-colored cocktail evokes sumptuous vacations in the Palm Beach area of Florida.

PASSING THROUGH AN ORANGE GROVE,
FLORIDA

C.16—One of the World's Finest Hotels—The Breakers, at Palm Beach, Florida

Stately Royal Palms, Florida

COLONY CLUB, PALM BEACH, FLORIDA—57

Henry Flagler, a founder of Standard Oil and The Florida East Coast Railway, was responsible for developing Palm Beach as a playground for wealthy members of the Gilded Age. The Breakers Hotel in Palm Beach is a perfect place to enjoy this special cocktail. Built in 1926 by the heirs of Henry Flagler, no expense was spared constructing this marvelous structure inspired by the Villa Medici in Rome. Skilled artisans were brought in from Italy to decorate the high-arched ceilings with detailed paintings. The magnificent property, with its rich decor, landscaped patios, and comfortable terraces, became a fashionable destination for sophisticated travelers during the Palm Beach winter season.

During World War II, the hotel was stripped of its luxuries and utilized by the United States Army as a military hospital. Following World War II, plush details restored, cocktails could be enjoyed at The Breakers once more. A fitting tribute to the opulence of Flagler's resort, the Palm Beach Special is your ticket to seaside glamour and luxury.

☞ Palm Beach Special

2 ounces gin
½ ounce sweet vermouth
¾ ounce fresh grapefruit juice

Place all ingredients in a cocktail shaker with ice. Shake vigorously and strain into a chilled cocktail glass.

Miami Beach Cocktail

During Prohibition, alcohol was still legal in the Caribbean Islands, a convenient neighbor to Florida's shore. Whisky, vermouth, and liquor of all kinds were produced legally in other parts of the world, shipped to warehouses in the Caribbean, and then smuggled into Miami Beach's hotels and establishments. Enterprising entrepreneurs did not want their customers hopping on a boat to spend their money in Cuba or the Bahamas and eagerly awaited the illegal liquor. It seems only natural that grapefruit juice from Florida's citrus industry and the illicitly obtained whisky and vermouth combined to inspire this refreshing cocktail. The Miami Beach Cocktail is a product of South Florida's "liquid gold" trade during the Prohibition years.

"Rum-running"—the smuggling of prohibited liquor—was a dangerous business that involved transporting liquor across the sea, avoiding hijacking pirates, and dodging the American Coast Guard. Legendary rum-runner Marie Waite, infamously referred to as "Spanish Marie," was known for her beauty as well as her ruthlessness. Following the death of her husband in a shoot-out near Biscayne Bay, Waite took over the business of transporting contraband onto Florida's shore. An August 19, 1929 article in *The Pittsburgh Press* discusses the capture of "the notorious rum-running queen, Spanish Marie" in Miami's Coconut Grove. The account describes her successful plea to the arresting officers, persuading them to send her home at once to tend to her "sleeping babies." She was released on a $500 dollar bond, never appeared in court, and became as obscure as her rum-running empire.

Miami Beach became a popular tourist destination, offering visitors an exotic tropical atmosphere, nightclubs, and sandy beaches. In the 1930s and 1940s, pastel-colored, streamlined buildings sprang up along the shore, defining a unique collection of Art Deco hotels and structures. Many remain standing and Miami Beach's South Beach was placed on the National Register of Historic Places. Highlighted by turquoise ocean views, pink sand, and swaying palm trees, hotels such as the Victor (1937), Clevelander (1938), Cardozo (1939), and Delano (1947) offer authentic vintage glamour

FIVE O'CLOCK CLUB COLLINS AVE. AT 22ND ST. MIAMI BEACH, FLORIDA
COCKTAIL LOUNGE

of a time gone by. One can sip the Miami Beach Cocktail while imagining the intrigue of seafaring adventures, smuggled booze, and the elegance of the Art Deco age.

☞ Miami Beach Cocktail

¾ ounce whisky (Scotch)
¾ ounce dry vermouth
¾ ounce fresh white grapefruit juice

Place all ingredients in a cocktail shaker filled with ice, shake, and strain into a chilled cocktail glass.

FIVE O'CLOCK CLUB   COLLINS AVE. AT 22ND ST.   MIAMI BEACH, FLORIDA

COCKTAIL LOUNGE   6A-H2852

By "Streamliner" Thru Tropical Florida

Technology and the Revolving Bar:

Bars from the 1930s—40s

Technological advances abounded in the 1930s and were incorporated into the entertainment, food, and beverage industries. Innovations such as revolving food counters allowed seated customers to grab their meals as they passed them by. In 1932, Radio City Music Hall, part of Rockefeller Center in New York City, opened with a ground-breaking stage incorporating hydraulic lifts and rotational features that enabled fantastic staging options and dazzling shows. So advanced were these features that access to the workings of the stage were reportedly guarded by the military during World War II to ensure spies would not steal the technology.

154:—RADIO CITY MUSIC HALL, WORLD'S LARGEST THEATRE, NEW YORK CITY.

42130

MERRY-GO-ROUND CAFE

MERRY GO ROUND

The Restaurant of Unique Service

171 O'Farrell St. ~ San Francisco, Calif.

It wasn't long after Prohibition ended that advances in rotational capabilities were expanded to create the revolving bar. The Merry-Go-Round bar became the hit draw that barkeeps longed to install for their thrill-seeking customers. The concept was so engaging that establishments grand and modest, in cities big and small, embraced it.

"THE NATION'S SMARTEST THEATRE RESTAURANT"   WHERE THE BAR REVOLVES

CHEZ AMI ~ 311 DELAWARE AVENUE ~ BUFFALO, N.Y.

One of the earliest Merry-Go-Round bars was located at the Congress Hotel in Chicago, Illinois. An announcement in the *Chicago Tribune* on May 12, 1933, stated, "While the hurdy-gurdy played old favorites like 'Sweet Adeline,' 50 or more persons found footing at the polished rail of a merry-go-round bar yesterday in the Pompeian room of the Congress Hotel." The announcement claimed that the new revolving bar was the second in the country, the first being in New York. Future advertisements encouraged customers to stop by for wonderful food and music and the opportunity to "ride while you drink."

The Copley Plaza Hotel in Boston, Massachusetts followed suit and installed its Merry-Go-Round bar in 1934. The Copley Plaza,

MERRY-GO-ROUND BAR — RITZ CARLTON HOTEL — ATLANTIC CITY, NEW JERSEY

known for its elegance, added a touch of playfulness to usher in a new era of nightlife after the repeal of Prohibition. A popular place with Bostonians and tourists alike, the Merry-Go-Round bar at the Copley was famous in its time as the destination for a special evening.

Atlantic City, New Jersey, was home to another well-known Merry-Go-Round bar. Located in the Ritz-Carlton Hotel on the boardwalk, it was touted as "a unique rendezvous where there is dancing during cocktail hour, dinner and supper, the year-round." Drinks flowed freely in Atlantic City during Prohibition thanks to long-time resident of the Ritz-Carlton, Boss "Nucky" Johnson. With links to organized crime, Johnson made sure whiskey, wine, women, and slot machines were available at the seaside resort. His pointed rationale for the illegal amenities was, "If people didn't want it, it wouldn't exist."

The rotational-themed bar could be spotted at many nightclubs and lounges in diverse cities across the country. The Chez Ami in Buffalo, New York, served its customers at a revolving bar, whereas the Blue Mirror in Washington, DC used a clever twist by placing its orchestra on a revolving stage. Not to be left out of the fun, by the 1940s, the Fairmont

MERRY-GO-ROUND BAR, POMPEIAN ROOM — CONGRESS HOTEL — CHICAGO

Hotel in San Francisco, California, as well as the Monteleone Hotel in New Orleans, Louisiana, added their own revolving bars.

The Merry-Go-Round themed bars capture the spirit of the golden age of nightclubs, lounges, and bars of the post-Prohibition years. During the Great Depression, throughout World War II, and into the prosperous post-war years, America's drinking culture evolved and thrived. As a tribute to the whimsical revolving bars of the 1930s and 1940s, enjoy the Merry-Go-Round Cocktail, created by Douglass Miller, Certified Wine and Spirits Specialist.

Merry-Go-Round Cocktail

1½ ounces rye whiskey
¾ ounce Yellow Chartreuse
¾ ounce dry vermouth
¾ ounce fresh lemon juice
Lemon wheel, for garnish

Place all of the ingredients in a cocktail shaker filled with ice and shake until cold. Strain the contents into a chilled cocktail glass and garnish with a lemon wheel.

South

Souvenir Folder of NEW ORLEANS LOUISIANA

POSTAGE 1½ ¢ WITHOUT MESSAGE

CANAL STREET BY NIGHT

Sazerac

New Orleans, Louisiana, is home to one of America's oldest cocktails, the Sazerac. A complex layering of ingredients, the Sazerac has evolved over time resulting in a strong and sophisticated cocktail with a history as interesting as the city itself. The earliest version of the drink was made with Sazerac de Forge et Fils, a cognac imported to an establishment opened in 1859 in the city known as the "Big Easy." Peychaud's bitters, which were produced in a New Orleans' apothecary, was initially added to the cognac, making it a medicinal tonic, tasty enough to be enjoyed even in good health. Over time, absinthe was added to the cocktail and in subsequent years the cognac was replaced with rye whiskey and a touch of sugar.

The Roosevelt Hotel in New Orleans has remained a splendid place to enjoy this fine cocktail. The hotel opened in 1923, offering superior amenities to an A-list clientele including US presidents, European royalty, and famous celebrities. Former

Louisiana governor and US Senator Huey P. Long, the "King-fish," chose the Roosevelt as his preferred lodging. During the 1930s, he reportedly had the Airline Highway constructed to shorten his trip from the State Capitol in Baton Rouge directly to his cherished hotel. The hotel's famed supper club, the Blue Room, opened on New Year's Eve in 1935. It quickly became recognized as one of the city's premiere venues for music, featuring entertainers such as Louis Armstrong, Ella Fitzgerald, Tommy Dorsey, Frank Sinatra, and Sammy Kaye. History was made at the hotel in 1949 when women stormed the Sazerac Bar successfully abolishing the long-maintained "men only" policy. The Sazerac Bar, with its long walnut counter, and the elegant Blue Room, continue to serve happy patrons this historical cocktail. Both the Roosevelt Hotel and the Sazerac cocktail have withstood the test of time.

Try this version of the Sazerac from the 1938 cocktail book, *Famous New Orleans Cocktails and How to Mix 'Em.*

BLUE ROOM, THE ROOSEVELT, NEW ORLEANS, LOUISIANA

Home of the Famous

BLUE ROOM

Dining and Dancing

"PRIDE OF THE SOUTH"

NEW ORLEANS

Sazerac

1 cube sugar
2 dashes Peychaud's bitters
1 dash Angostura bitters
2 ounces rye whiskey
Splash of absinthe
Twist of lemon

Place the sugar cube and a few drops of water in a heavy mixing glass and crush the sugar cube until it dissolves. Add Peychaud's bitters, Angostura bitters, rye whiskey, a few pieces of ice, and stir. Coat the interior of a chilled heavy-bottomed glass with absinthe, drain off the excess. Strain the contents from the mixing glass into the chilled, absinthe-coated glass. Twist the lemon peel over the top.

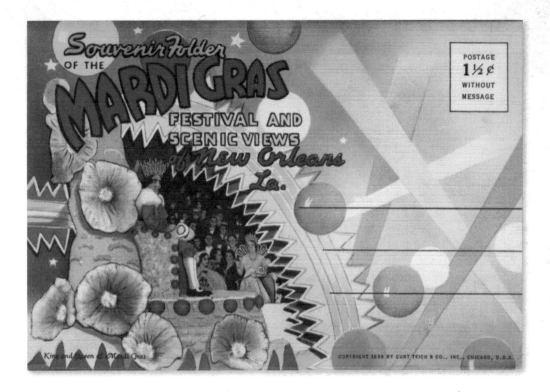

Ramos Gin Fizz

The Ramos Gin Fizz is one of many classic drinks ensconced in New Orleans cocktail history. Created by Henry C. Ramos in 1888 at the Imperial Cabinet Saloon, this well-guarded recipe was later recreated at Ramos' own bar, the Stag, which opened in 1907. After the repeal of Prohibition, the recipe was revived by Ramos' brother and trademarked to the Roosevelt Hotel in New Orleans. The frothy appeal of the drink is achieved through vigorous shaking, enhancing the delicately flavored ingredients. Popular during Mardi Gras, several "shaker boys" were hired to keep up with the demand.

The Ramos Gin Fizz was a favorite of "Kingfish" Huey P. Long, famed Louisiana governor and US Senator. The former governor set up headquarters in his private suite at the Roosevelt Hotel and frequently enjoyed his Ramos Gin Fizz at the bar. Long visited the bar at the Hotel New Yorker during a trip

179

LOUISIANA'S TWO GREATEST MONUMENTS, CONCEIVED AND BUILT BY THE LATE U. S. SENATOR HUEY P. LONG

STATE CAPITOL, BATON ROUGE

NEW HUEY P. LONG BRIDGE, NEW ORLEANS

Greetings from LOUISIANA

to New York City in 1935. As a publicity stunt he had his favorite bartender, Sam Guarino from the Roosevelt Hotel, flown in to teach the bartender at the Hotel New Yorker the proper execution of his beloved drink. After sampling the results, the Kingfish proclaimed the properly constructed Ramos Gin Fizz his "gift to New York," and the event was recorded on newsreel.

Although the colorful and progressive Louisiana politician was assassinated later that year, it is worthwhile to take the time to mix this cocktail, slow down, and think about times gone by.

☞ Ramos Gin Fizz

1 egg white
2 ounces gin
1 ounce half-and-half cream
Juice of ½ lemon
Juice of ½ lime
2 or 3 drops orange flower water
Touch of superfine sugar
Splash of seltzer

Place the egg white in the cocktail shaker and dry shake vigorously until the egg white becomes frothy. Add ice and all other ingredients in the shaker except for the seltzer and continue to shake vigorously. This may take a few minutes. When completed, place in a tall glass with a splash of seltzer for added fizz.

✳ ***Note:*** *Generously sized ice cubes can help achieve the proper consistency of this drink.*

Brulatour Courtyard, 520 Royal Street
New Orleans, La.   19

Vieux Carré Cocktail

During the Great Depression, Walter Bergeron, head bartender at the Hotel Monteleone in New Orleans, invented this strong and potent drink. Sure to make one forget their troubles, he

CAROUSEL LOUNGE IN HOTEL MONTELEONE

NEW ORLEANS, LA.

named it the Vieux Carré in honor of the hotel's location. Vieux Carré means "Old Square" and refers to one of New Orleans' oldest and most romantic neighborhoods, the French Quarter.

Originally built in 1886 and purchased by cobbler Antonio Monteleone, the Hotel Monteleone has remained in family ownership for five generations. Maintaining an opulent Beaux Arts style through several expansions, the hotel has earned the title "Grand Dame of the French Quarter."

A popular destination of many literary greats, past guests included Ernest Hemingway, William Faulkner, and Tennessee Williams. Hemingway mentioned the Hotel Monteleone in his short story, "Night Before Battle," and Williams in his play, *The Rose Tattoo*. One of Truman Capote's favorite hotels, he liked to boast he was born at the Monteleone, but in truth his mother was living at the

COURTYARD, LITTLE THEATRE,
NEW ORLEANS, LA.

hotel during her pregnancy and brought to the hospital in time for his birth. Due to its elite literary distinction, the Friends of the Library Association declared the Hotel Monteleone an official literary landmark.

Another outstanding feature of the Hotel Monteleone is the Carousel Bar. Built in 1949, the bar revolves slowly, completing one revolution every fifteen minutes. Patrons enjoying the rich and complex flavors of the Vieux Carré Cocktail can barely feel the motion. The cocktail is meant to be savored, and is a great homage to this historic hotel and its distinguished literary guests.

Vieux Carré Cocktail

Bénédictine rinse
2 dashes Peychaud's bitters
2 dashes Angostura bitters
1 ounce rye whiskey
1 ounce cognac
¾ ounce sweet vermouth
Cherry, for garnish
Lemon twist, for garnish

Coat the interior of a chilled rock glass with Bénédictine and add Peychaud's bitters and Angostura bitters. Add rye whiskey, cognac, sweet vermouth, and one ice cube into the glass. Stir ingredients gently for a few seconds. You may garnish with a cherry and lemon twist. Sip slowly and enjoy.

Willard Room
WILLARD HOTEL — WASHINGTON, D.C.

Mint Julep

What comes to mind when you think of a Mint Julep? The Kentucky Derby, of course! This refreshing mint and bourbon fare was first served at Churchill Downs, home of the Kentucky Derby racetrack, around 1875. The Mint Julep became the Derby's official drink in 1938. A year later, Churchill Downs and the Libbey Glass Company created souvenir glasses that were an instant hit and highly collectible, increasing sales of the drink threefold. The president of the track introduced a sterling silver cup with a horseshoe embellishment in 1951. Also popular at that time was a rhythm and blues song entitled "One Mint Julep" by The Clovers. A woeful young man sings about how drinking one Mint Julep was the cause of it all—a stolen kiss, a shotgun wedding, and six kids!

Many states lay claim to the creation of this drink, including Maryland, Pennsylvania, Mississippi, and Virginia. It was Senator Henry Clay of Kentucky, who introduced the beverage to

Two Typical Kentuckians
Personality and Mint Julep
Relics almost extinct—
K28

Souvenir of the Kentucky Derby, Churchill Downs, Louisville, Ky.

Washington, DC, sometime around 1820 at the Round Robin Bar at Tennison's Hotel, a pre-cursor to the landmark Willard Hotel. Senator Clay engaged in a persuasive discussion with Captain Frederick Marryat, a British naval hero and author, whether to use rum, brandy, or bourbon. Clay produced his diary indicating the use of bourbon, which is now considered the definitive alcohol of choice.

While the Kentucky Derby is thought to be the most exciting two minutes in sports, one can savor the Mint Julep by sipping it slowly and enjoying it anytime of the year.

☞ Mint Julep

8–10 mint leaves
1 teaspoon sugar plus more for dusting
2 ounces bourbon
Soda water
Mint sprig, for garnish
Lemon twist, for garnish

Place the mint leaves, sugar, and a small measure of bourbon in a glass. Muddle with spoon. Half fill the glass with ice and gently agitate the mixture. Fill with remaining ice, add the rest of the bourbon, and top of with soda water. Garnish with fresh sprig of mint and a twist of lemon. Gently dust with sugar.

Bred in Old Kentucky, Man O' War, the Wonder Horse

814—Ranch Home of Mr. and Mrs. Clark Gable (Carole Lombard), Encino, California

Scarlett O'Hara Cocktail

Margaret Mitchell's book, *Gone with the Wind*, published in 1936, became an unprecedented success, earning a Pulitzer Prize in 1937. Mitchell, born in Atlanta, Georgia, set her romantic novel during the Civil War and told her story from a Southern point of view. An interview conducted on July 13, 1936, by Mitchell's former colleague, Medora Perkerson from the *Atlanta Journal*, was broadcast over radio station WSB in Atlanta. During the interview, Mitchell discusses the elements that provided inspiration for *Gone with the Wind*. One important influence occurred during her childhood visits to family and friends where she was exposed to the old gentleman who had served in the Confederate Army. She was so fascinated by their debates she was later shocked to find out that the South had lost the war! These accounts, combined with Atlanta's role in the Civil War, provided the backdrop for a story she felt had not been told.

Mitchell weaves a complex tapestry intertwining the novel's characters, their relationships, and their response to the hardships of war. The heroine, Scarlett O'Hara, is changed by the effects of war from a spoiled and selfish young woman to a formidable adventuress. Conversely, the novel's dashing hero, Captain Rhett Butler, joined the Confederate Army only when he was sure they would lose and proposed making money out of the wrecking of the Confederacy. Mitchell describes the central theme of her novel as a theme of survival.

The movie rights for *Gone with the Wind* were sold for $50,000 to producer David O. Selznick in 1936. The four-hour-long Technicolor film premiered at Atlanta's Loew's Grand Theatre on December 15, 1939. The movie, casting Clark Gable as Rhett Butler and Vivien Leigh as Scarlett O'Hara, was met with great fanfare throughout the city. On opening night, actress Hattie McDaniel, who played the part of a black

795 HOME OF CLARK GABLE, BRENTWOOD HIGHLANDS, CALIF.

2027 AZALEA TIME IN FLORIDA

servant in the production, was not permitted to attend due to the Jim Crow laws. Gable was so incensed at the treatment of his friend he threatened not to attend the premier and did so only at McDaniel's insistence. In 1940, McDaniel changed history when she won an Oscar for her supporting role in *Gone with the Wind*, becoming the first black entertainer to achieve this honor.

The nation was enthralled with *Gone with the Wind* and its heroine, generating Scarlett O'Hara handkerchiefs, statues, playing cards, and a namesake cocktail! Versions of the red-tinged cocktail appeared shortly after the opening of the film. The recipe below is from *Trader Vic's Book of Food and Drink* (1946).

 Scarlett O'Hara Cocktail

1½ ounces Southern Comfort
1 ounce cranberry juice
1 dash fresh lime juice

Place ingredients into a cocktail shaker filled with ice, shake, and strain into a cocktail glass.

the "BATTLE OF ATLANTA"

Exterior of Cyclorama, which houses the painting

ATLANTA, GEORGIA

Big Bands and Swing Music:

Trends from the mid-1930s—40s

Following the stock market crash of 1929, Americans had little money to spend on entertainment. Families enjoyed gathering around their radio sets to listen to their favorite shows. The concept of "installment buying" made radio sets affordable during the Great Depression, providing a welcome diversion during difficult times. By 1939, American households had an estimated 28,000,000 sets. Radio broadcasting developed by leaps and bounds through linking radio stations across the nation by telephone wire. This chain broadcasting technique allowed radio shows to be heard coast to coast.

The EMPIRE ROOM of the PALMER HOUSE in CHICAGO

Band Shell at Concert Grounds, Allen "A" Resort, Wolfeboro, N. H.

ALLEN "A" RESORT

Thanks to the popularity of radio and the advancement of broadcasting technology, big band "swing" music spread across the country. Swing was the dominant style of popular music that swept the nation from 1935 to 1945. The lively tempo and strong rhythm of swing made it a compelling choice as dance music. A typical swing piece includes elements of improvisation with a soloist taking center stage while the rest of the band plays support. As the song progresses, multiple soloists take their turn in the spotlight. Big bands frequently featured vocalists, which helped develop the careers of performers such as Ella Fitzgerald, Peggy Lee, and Frank Sinatra.

Bands often owed their success to the radio broadcasts of their live events across the country. In 1934, Benny Goodman's band was featured weekly on NBC's radio program

PLEASE MAESTRO PLAY

THIS LITTLE NUMBER

Please give this request to your Waiter

★ ★ ★

NAME ....

ADDRESS ....

....

TERRACE RESTAURANT   HOTEL NEW YORKER

THE COLISEUM
PARKERSBURG
W. VA.

WEST VIRGINIA'S
LARGEST AND FINEST

BALLROOM

COLISEUM ORCHESTRA "CHUCK" DROLLINGER, DIRECTOR — PLAYING EVERY SATURDAY   4A-H317

Let's Dance. By 1936, Tommy Dorsey's band had a national radio presence broadcasting from Dallas, and later from Los Angeles. From 1939 until 1942, Glenn Miller and His Orchestra were featured three times a week on radio broadcasts from CBS.

America loved to dance in the Big Band era. Ballrooms such as the Palomar in Los Angeles and the Savoy in New York were filled to capacity with couples dancing the Lindy Hop, Suzy-Q, and the Big Apple. The Savoy Ballroom, operating from 1926 until 1958, featured the popular "Battle of the Bands" competition in its huge space. Chick Webb's band was the reigning king at the Savoy's competitions, famously beating Count Basie's, as well as Benny Goodman's band. The Savoy's customer policy was unusual for the time,

allowing white and black bands to perform to a mixed audience.

The Cotton Club in New York City was one of the premier places to go for hot jazz. Opening in 1923, the venue was operated by gangster Owney Madden, who made sure the booze flowed freely during the Prohibition years. The club continued to offer an impressive list of spirits after repeal. Fashionably dressed white patrons made their way to the Cotton Club, which featured all black musicians, dancers, and entertainers. The talent at the Cotton Club was unsurpassed, and included jazz greats Fletcher Henderson, Duke Ellington, and Cab Calloway. Radio broadcasts direct from the Cotton Club brought attention to Duke Ellington's music, and helped promote the sale of his recordings.

Posh supper clubs across the country presented radio broadcasts of big band performances during the height of swing music's popularity. In 1935, Benny Goodman's band opened in the newly designed Joseph Urban room at Chicago's Congress Hotel, featuring live broadcasts during their six-month engagement. For many years, big band music drifted over the airwaves from the Hotel New Yorker's famed Terrace Room. Here a patron might slip a request written on the hotel's special form to maestro Sammy Kaye with hopes of hearing the band play one of his or her favorite "swing and sway" numbers.

During the Great Depression and World War II, Americans tuned in to hear big band music from venues large and small, famous and less known. Dining, dancing, and drinking, while listening to live big band performances, was a way to cope with the challenging circumstances of the time.

Big Band trumpeter Harry James' "Get off the Stand" number provided the inspiration for this distinctive recipe. The Get Off the Stand Cocktail captures the effervescent Big Band Era and was created by Frank Caiafa, author of *The Waldorf Astoria Bar Book* (2016), and principal at Handle Bars NYC Inc.

SAVOY BALLROOM —— Lenox Avenue and 140th Street —— NEW YORK

BALINESE ROOM — THE BLACKSTONE HOTEL — CHICAGO

NO COVER CHARGE
DEL COURTNEY
AND HIS ORCHESTRA
FLOOR SHOW

FAMOUS for FOOD and ENTERTAINMENT

The **BLACKHAWK** *Restaurant*

RANDOLPH AT WABASH ● CHICAGO

TULANE ROOM
JUNG HOTEL
On Famed Canal St., New Orleans

☞ Get Off the Stand Cocktail

2 ounces flavorful white rum
1½ ounces Byrrh Grand Quinquina
1/3 ounce fresh lemon juice
3 dashes chocolate bitters
2 ounces chilled club soda
Lemon twist, for garnish

Add all ingredients to a mixing glass, except club soda, add ice, and shake well. Strain into a Collins glass filled with large ice cubes. Top with club soda and stir to integrate. Twist a lemon peel on top to release oils and top as the garnish.

COCKTAIL LOUNGE AND SAPPHIRE BAR

CHEZ PAREE, 610 FAIRBANKS COURT, CHICAGO, ILL.

... for glamour and gayety ...

El Dorado

COCKTAIL
LOUNGE
and DINING ROOM

COMMODORE PERRY HOTEL
TOLEDO, OHIO

HOE SAI GAI MODERN ROOM

85 W. RANDOLPH ST. — CHICAGO, ILL.

9A415

Midwest

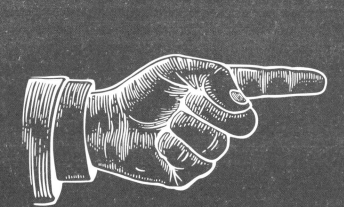

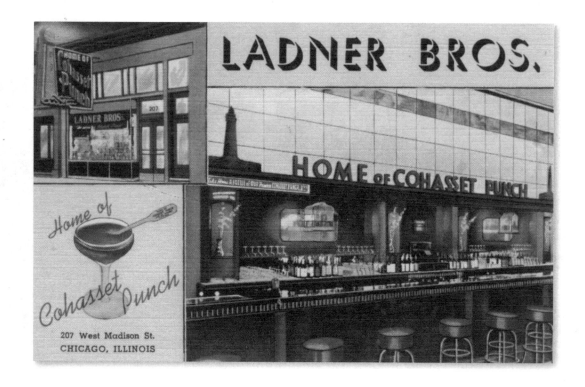

207 West Madison St.
CHICAGO, ILLINOIS

Cohasset Punch

Chicago's Ladner brothers reopened their saloon after Prohibition ended in 1934. The neon sign over the door announced that it was the "Home of the Cohasset Punch," with its accompanying lighthouse icon. Bartenders sported white shirts and ties and served the punch in the Ladner's own custom-designed glasses with a three-drink limit. Canaries in cages lined the walls, chirps becoming sweeter with each drink. The enterprising brothers bottled the Cohasset Punch for customers to take home, with instructions on the label for serving an individual, a dinner crowd, or a large reception.

The Ladner brothers originally bought the Cohasset Punch recipe from the Chicago restaurant Williams & Newman in 1916. Local liquor distributors at the time advertised that, "it braces one's nervous and physical system like a new elixir of life—better than a rare old wine." The drink was first created for William H. Crane, a noted actor who enjoyed a magnificent fifty-year acting career at the turn of the century. When Crane arranged fashionable summer parties at his home in Cohasset, Massachusetts, he brought bartender Gus Williams to make and serve the drinks. Williams created an original "thirst quencher" using the syrup from a can of peaches. The drink, called the Cohasset Punch, became the hit of the season and was later served at the Williams & Newman Restaurant. When the restaurant closed, Mrs. Newman sold the recipe to the Ladners. The Ladner Brothers' lighthouse symbol was taken from Minot's Ledge Lighthouse in Massachusetts' Cohasset Harbor and used on all promotional materials for their saloon.

The Cohasset Punch was a popular cocktail in its day. It appeared in a scene in Saul Bellow's first novel published in 1944, *The Dangling Man*, when he described a room: ". . . the light furniture in the popular Swedish style, the brown carpet, the Chagall and Gris prints, the vines trailing from the mantelpiece, the bowl of Cohasset punch." Although the recipe was highly guarded in a bank vault, the Edgewater Beach Hotel on the shores of Lake Michigan served the same exact drink in the 1950s, calling it the Edgewater Beach Cocktail. Enjoy the intriguing combination of a peach reposing in a spicy citrus blend of liquor and juices.

 ## Cohasset Punch

1 canned peach half, reserving ½ ounce of syrup
1½ ounces dark rum
1½ ounces vermouth (sweet or dry)
Juice of ½ lemon
1–2 dashes orange bitters

Place peach half in flat champagne glass. Fill glass halfway with shaved ice. Add liquids and stir. Top with the reserved syrup from the can.

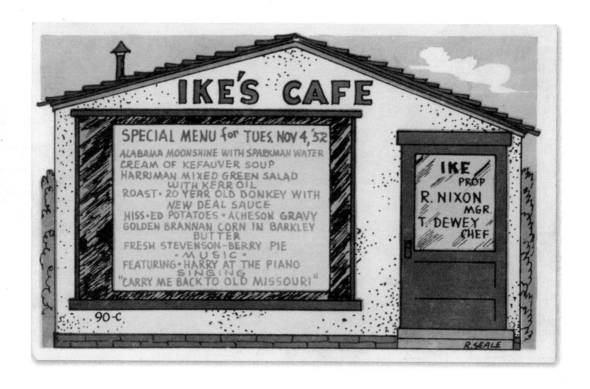

Inside the image:
IKE'S CAFE

SPECIAL MENU for TUES. NOV 4, '52
ALABAMA MOONSHINE WITH SPARKMAN WATER
CREAM OF KEFAUVER SOUP
HARRIMAN MIXED GREEN SALAD
    WITH KERR OIL
ROAST • 20 YEAR OLD DONKEY WITH
    NEW DEAL SAUCE
HISS • ED POTATOES • ACHESON GRAVY
GOLDEN BRANNAN CORN IN BARKLEY
    BUTTER
FRESH STEVENSON • BERRY PIE
    • M U S I C •
FEATURING • HARRY AT THE PIANO
    SINGING
"CARRY ME BACK TO OLD MISSOURI"

90-C

IKE
    PROP
R. NIXON
    MGR.
T. DEWEY
    CHEF

R. SEALE

Salty Dog

Chicago was bustling with activity in the heat of summer 1952. The Chicago International Amphitheater hosted both the Republican and Democratic Conventions, on July 7–11 and July 21–26 respectively. Tens of thousands of people poured into the city to join in the spectacle. Convention-goers filled hotels around the city, while delegates gathered at the Conrad Hilton Hotel for press conferences, photo shoots, and appearances on TV and radio. Well-wishers stormed the Hilton and enjoyed free soda.

The Amphitheater was originally home to the International Livestock Exhibition. It became the country's leading convention center after it was renovated to include comfortable seating and luxurious air conditioning. For the first time in broadcasting history, all major and independent radio and television stations were able to transmit the conventions into homes due to state-of-the-art technology installed at the amphitheater. Over seventy million people watched the proceedings on sixteen million television sets across America.

It was during the Republican Convention that George Jessel, entertainer and "Toastmaster General of the United States," claimed to have created the Salty Dog cocktail. The Republicans were trying to stop the twenty-year tide of democratic rule and wanted the best candidate to win the election. A bitter and tumultuous contest ensued between presidential nominees Dwight Eisenhower, a popular World War II general, and Ohio Senator Robert Taft. Taft was an isolationist and a conservative. Eisenhower was a moderate and wanted the United States to be more involved in world and social policy issues, such as resisting Soviet aggression in Europe and Asia, and accepting New Deal social welfare programs. The Republican Party, after four days of fistfights, hissing, chanting, mass demonstrating, jeers, and howls, selected General Dwight Eisenhower and Richard Nixon as the presidential and vice presidential candidates.

THE BOULEVARD ROOM

THE
Conrad Hilton
CHICAGO, ILLINOIS

Inez Robb, a nationally syndicated columnist, was covering the Convention when, at the Pump Room at the Ambassador East Hotel in Chicago, Jessel handed her a champagne glass. It was filled with his Salty Dog concoction of half fresh grapefruit juice, half vodka, and a dash of salt. He said that it "fortified him against the Republicans . . . and made you think any Democrat can win." While Jessel's recipe calls for a 50/50 combo, try this modified version if you don't want to start seeing double!

 # Salty Dog

Lime wedge
Kosher or sea salt
1½ ounces vodka
4 ounces fresh grapefruit juice
Lime, for garnish

Moisten rim of a highball glass with lime wedge. Dip rim into the salt to lightly coat. Add ice cubes, vodka, and juice. Garnish with lime.

103—View of International Amphitheatre taken from Inside of Yards Showing the Sirloin Club, Chicago

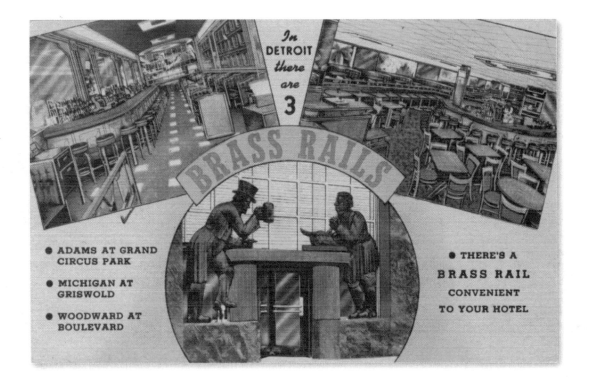

In DETROIT there are 3

BRASS RAILS

ADAMS AT GRAND
CIRCUS PARK

MICHIGAN AT
GRISWOLD

WOODWARD AT
BOULEVARD

THERE'S A

BRASS RAIL
CONVENIENT
TO YOUR HOTEL

The Last Word

In the early half of the twentieth century, Detroit, Michigan, emerged as America's automotive capital. As workers from the south streamed into the city seeking employment in the burgeoning car business, they brought with them jazz music. Earning the nickname the Motor City, and simply shortened to Motown, Detroit became as famous for its music as for its automobile production.

The Detroit Athletic Club (DAC), located across the street from the former Madison and Lenox Hotels, is one of the city's most prestigious private clubs. The clubhouse, with its fine appointments, garnered national attention at its opening in 1915. Automobile titans, captains of industry, and prominent athletes frequented the DAC. During the 1920s and 1930s, society's elite would listen to jazz orchestras under the auspices of the DAC's personal music director, impresario Jean Goldkette.

219— JAMES SCOTT MEMORIAL FOUNTAIN BY ILLUMINATION, BELLE ISLE PARK, DETROIT, MICH.

209— EDISON MEMORIAL FOUNTAIN, GRAND CIRCUS PARK, DETROIT, MICH.

As industry leaders mixed business with pleasure at the DAC, factory workers, as well as the middle class, found entertainment at clubs located in Detroit's Paradise Valley. During the 1920s, 1930s, 1940s, and 1950s, Paradise Valley and nearby ballrooms hosted some of the hottest acts in jazz and blues. Performers such as McKinney's Cotton Pickers, Leroy Smith and His Orchestra, Billie Holiday, Ella Fitzgerald, and Duke Ellington were part of the all-star line up, further ensconcing Detroit in music history.

A truly harmonious libation, The Last Word was not created by a musician, but rather a vaudevillian named Frank Fogarty. While visiting the DAC, Fogarty composed the cocktail by blending gin, Green Chartreuse liqueur, Maraschino liqueur, and lime juice, in four equal parts. The cocktail's pleasing pale green color, exotic flavor, and fresh herb-infused taste is a perfect way to reflect on Detroit's fascinating cultural history.

☞ The Last Word

¾ *ounce gin*
¾ *ounce Green Chartreuse*
¾ *ounce Maraschino liqueur*
¾ *ounce fresh lime juice*
Lime slice, for garnish (optional)
Maraschino cherry, for garnish (optional)

Place all ingredients in a cocktail shaker filled with ice. Shake and strain into a chilled cocktail glass. Add a slice of lime and a maraschino cherry, if desired.

A.2   MUNICIPAL BUILDINGS AND A. I. U. CITADEL, COLUMBUS, OHIO

6A-H2807

Mañana Cocktail

A time capsule was discovered in the rubble at the razed site of the Deshler Hotel in Columbus, Ohio. Among the items in the capsule was a letter from the owner, John Deshler, to the future citizens of Columbus. His words were full of prophesy about the future of his beloved city. He was keenly aware that his hotel would become obsolete and replaced with something more fitting for modern times. Indeed it did!

The 400-room Deshler Hotel, built in 1914, was considered to be the world's largest hotel and made of the finest materials and engineering feats of its day. It was replete with luxurious furnishings and decorations: Greek marble, French crystal, Spanish leather, and English silver. Lou Wallick was entreated to oversee the construction of the hotel and consequently leased it for twenty-five years. Incidentally, he was also the owner of the Hotel Wallick in New York, where Hugo Ensslin served as head bartender while he wrote the 1916 *Recipes for Mixed Drinks* book.

A8 Deshler Wallick Hotel, R. K. O. Theatre and A. I. U. Citadel,

Columbus, Ohio

In 1924, the Deshler needed to expand its operations. John Lentz, the founder of the American Insurance Union (AIU), also needed larger quarters for his company, as did the Keith Theaters (later known as RKO), who wanted to provide an elegant movie house for larger audiences. The three businesses created a comprehensive plan to enlarge the hotel to 1,000 rooms, build a palatial theater, and create an office tower as a citadel to the socialistic ideals of the AIU.

The multipurposed complex was the first of its type in an urban setting. The AIU citadel became the largest building in Ohio, the fifth tallest in the world, and half a foot taller than the Washington Monument. Influenced by his world travels and excessive wealth, Lentz spared no expense on decor. He mixed old styles with modern ones, and icons from the East and the West. The Palace Theater's design was fashioned after Versailles and seated over 2,800 patrons. The tower flaunted statuary, stained glass, bronze medallions, gold-plated fixtures, murals, fountains, and a massive pipe organ.

In the hotel, guests walked across a Venetian Bridge to dine at the ornate Pompeian, Ionian, or Spanish Rooms. It was in the Spanish Room, styled like a Sevillian castle, that Senator and Mrs. Taft hosted the "Taft-for-President" Executive Committee in preparation for the 1940 Republican Convention. Herb Smith, barman in the Spanish Room, created the Mañana Cocktail. David Embury, author of *The Fine Art of Mixing Drinks*, considered Smith to be one of the finest bartenders he had met since the repeal of Prohibition.

 Mañana Cocktail

3 ounces white rum
1 ounce apricot liqueur
½ ounce fresh lemon juice
½ ounce grenadine

Shake in a cocktail shaker with finely crushed ice and strain into a chilled cocktail glass.

HOTEL MUEHLEBACH — KANSAS CITY, MISSOURI   2A-H306.

Rendezvous Cocktail

A huge snowstorm raged outside as four men remained stranded in the lobby of the Muehlebach Hotel in Kansas City, Missouri, in late March 1938. In the true spirit of making the best of a situation, they began to sing and harmonize. This chance meeting would lead to the formation of the Barbershop Harmony Society, an international group of barbershop singers. It was here at the Muehlebach Hotel that the Rendezvous Cocktail was created.

The Muehlebach family, founders of their namesake beer company, built the hotel in 1915. A prestigious guest list included many US presidents and the penthouse suite served as headquarters for President Harry S. Truman when he was in town. Truman often stayed at the hotel en route to his home in Independence, Missouri. As the incumbent, Truman

maintained his optimism while waiting for results at the Muehlebach Hotel on Election Day, November 2, 1948. It was on this day he won the US presidency against Thomas E. Dewey, in what is considered the greatest election upset in American history.

Famous for presidential and harmonizing guests, the Muehlebach Hotel offered several glamorous venues such as the Terrace Grill and the Rendezvous. This signature cocktail is a combination of gin, Maraschino liqueur, and lime juice, and is most likely named for the hotel's Rendezvous Restaurant. True to Missourian character, the Rendezvous is straightforward and unpretentious, yet clean and crisp like that long ago snowy night.

 ## Rendezvous Cocktail

1 ounce gin
½ ounce Maraschino liqueur
½ ounce fresh lime juice

Place all ingredients in a cocktail shaker filled with ice, shake vigorously, and strain into a chilled cocktail glass.

Club Continental

NEW HOTEL JEFFERSON · · · · SAINT LOUIS, MO.

Golden Glow Cocktail

The Jefferson Hotel in St. Louis, Missouri, opened on April 24, 1904, to accommodate visitors to the Louisiana Purchase Exposition. The Exposition, also known as the 1904 World's Fair, commemorated the centennial of the Louisiana Purchase of 1803. The fair's opening was pushed back to 1904, allowing full-scale participation of dignitaries from abroad.

The Jefferson Hotel, named in honor of Thomas Jefferson, was influenced by the architecture of the nation's finest hotels. It was projected to be "as handsome as the Waldorf–Astoria, NY." Located in St. Louis' downtown area, the hotel continued offering first-class accommodations after the fair's closing and was considered the city's premier hostelry. The hotel underwent construction in 1928, adding another 400 guest rooms, new banquet halls, and a state-of-the-art parking garage. The updated hotel became known as the New Jefferson Hotel.

As one of the nation's leading beer and wine producers in the United States, Missouri fostered a liberal attitude toward alcohol laws prior to Prohibition. The state rejected Prohibition on three separate initiative elections before it became part of the Constitution. When Temperance crusader Carrie A. Nation, known for smashing liquor bottles with a hatchet, entered a Missouri town in 1901, she was promptly arrested. The judge stayed her fine with the provision she leave Missouri and never return.

It's no surprise that St. Louis was ready to celebrate following the repeal of Prohibition. The New Jefferson Hotel did its best to welcome back its imbibing patrons in style by providing them top-notch cocktails with an array of fine ingredients. An advertisement in the *St. Louis Star and Times* on October 23, 1934, proclaims, "Tomorrow the sun will dawn upon a refreshingly modern, exotic type of cocktail lounge and tap room in St. Louis—The Rendezvous at the New Jefferson Hotel." The

The Rendezvous

NEW HOTEL JEFFERSON · · SAINT LOUIS, MO.

advertisement goes on to describe the vast selection of spirits that will be available to the discerning customer such as Milshire Gin, Gilbey's Spey Royal Scotch, Blue Ribbon Whiskey, and Old Hermitage.

The New Jefferson Hotel also offered St. Louis' "smartest entertainment" in its Club Continental, where revelers could dine, dance, and drink the "finest spirits." In its day, the New Jefferson Hotel was, "Where discriminating St. Louisans meet . . . discriminating St. Louisans."

 # Golden Glow Cocktail

1½ ounces bourbon whiskey
1 dash Jamaican rum
1½ ounces fresh orange juice
½ ounce fresh lemon juice
1 teaspoon fine sugar
Drop of grenadine

Place all ingredients into an electric blender with crushed ice, process, and strain into a hollow-stemmed champagne glass, which has a stem filled with grenadine.

✳ *Note: A drop of grenadine in the bottom of a non-hollow-stemmed champagne glass is also acceptable.*

Pink Squirrel

Sweet and nutty in flavor, this whimsical cocktail is sure to delight with its signature pink color. The Pink Squirrel is credited to mixologist Bryant Sharp, the original owner of Bryant's Cocktail Lounge in Milwaukee, Wisconsin. The novel ingredient in the cocktail is Crème de Noyaux. Not always easy to find but worth the hunt, the liqueur is made from the kernels of apricots and gives the drink its pink hue.

Bryant's Cocktail Lounge first opened in the 1930s as a "tied house" to the Miller Brewing Company. A tied house refers to a tavern or establishment linked to a brewery that sells their products. Milwaukee, known for its beer industry, had many of these taverns and they were part of the city's social culture. Bryant Sharp made the decision to transform his establishment into a cocktail lounge during this era. Touted as Milwaukee's first cocktail bar, the lounge was dark and swanky. Bryant's has changed hands, survived a devastating fire, and was restored

A Nut Cracker

LAKOTA'S
Theatre Restaurant
602-604 W. WISCONSIN AVE.
MILWAUKEE, WIS.

LAKOTA'S
RESTAURANT DANCING COCKTAIL BAR RESTAURANT DANCING

*The Biggest in the State
In the Heart of Milwaukee*

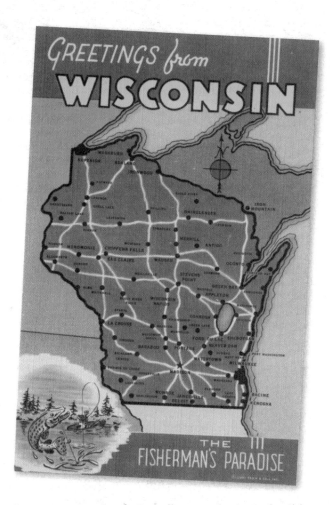

in the true spirit of a suave and atmospheric cocktail lounge. The Pink Squirrel is an amusing contribution to Milwaukee's cocktail culture.

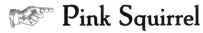 Pink Squirrel

¾ ounce Crème de Noyaux
¾ ounce white crème de cacao
1 ounce fresh half-and-half cream

Place all ingredients in a cocktail shaker with ice. Shake vigorously and strain into a cocktail glass.

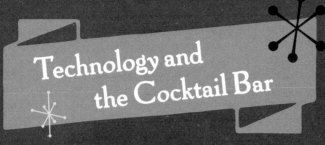

Technology and the Cocktail Bar

Ice-Skating Shows from the mid-1930s—50s

From the mid-1930s through the World War II years and beyond, ice-skating shows were immensely popular at supper clubs and other venues. The trend was first introduced in the early twentieth century at Hotel Sherman's College Inn and the Morrison Hotel, both located in Chicago, Illinois. Prohibition put an end to the dinner and ice-skating revues. However, after repeal, hotels reintroduced the concept with great success.

The first indoor refrigerated ice-skating rink, The Glaciarium, opened in Chelsea,

The New "ICE FOLLIES OF 1940", World's Greatest Musical Revue on Ice

London, in 1876. By 1879, New York City's Madison Square Garden had an indoor ice-skating rink and presented gas-lit shows to the delight of audiences. As electricity became more readily available, advances in refrigeration permitted the development of efficient systems to maintain the rink at a consistent temperature. Ice-skating rinks were developed in auditoriums for recreation, hockey, and ice shows.

The Ice Follies, founded by Shipstads and Johnson in 1936, was the first large-scale touring ice show. The Shipstad brothers and Oscar Johnson were talented ice-skaters and developed a successful formula of beautiful figure-skating acts and comedic ice-skating skits that appealed to audiences. *The Ice Capades*, another touring show, began in

1940, featuring ice-skating stars such as Dorothy Lewis, Donna Atwood, and Megan Taylor. Republic Pictures was intrigued by the Ice Capades and produced two movie pictures based on the company entitled *Ice Capades* (1941) and *Ice Capades Revue* (1942).

Sonja Henie, the Olympic ice-skating champion of 1928, 1932, and 1936, brought her talents to America, appearing in ice-skating revues and on Hollywood's silver screen. Her movies include such extravaganzas as *Thin Ice* (1937), *Second Fiddle* (1939), and *Sun Valley Serenade* (1941). Her popularity sparked an international interest in figure-skating and it was only a hop, skip, and a jump before enterprising hotels melded the indoor refrigerated rink into their supper club revues.

Numerous hotels across America installed

tiny ice rinks in their venues. Many of these rinks were only twenty feet by twenty feet and the ice-skating revues were referred to as "tank shows." Theatrical ice shows dazzled diners in cities from coast to coast. Patrons could dine, drink, and enjoy the magic of talented skaters twirling just feet away from their table. Venues such as the Roosevelt Hotel in New Orleans, Louisiana, the Nicollet Hotel in Minneapolis, Minnesota, the Conrad Hilton Hotel in Chicago, Illinois, and the St. Regis Hotel in New York, presented sparkling revues on stages of ice.

The Adolphus Hotel in Dallas, Texas, featured long running ice-skating revues with several shows a day. A novelty for Dallas' warm climate, the ice shows held special appeal. The performances were popular with the ladies lunch crowd and socialites could be seen enjoying the stunning ice shows in the hotel's sumptuously decorated Century Room, while sipping a champagne cocktail. Starting in 1943, Olympic speed-skater-turned-figure-skater Dot Franey staged and starred in her own show at the hotel. A real crowd-pleaser, *Dot Franey's Ice Time Revue* was so successful it was held over at the Adolphus for fourteen years.

The Hotel New Yorker located in New York City presented sensational ice-skating shows in its famed Terrace Room for many years. Norval Baptie and Gladys Lamb, a talented figure-skating couple, choreographed, staged, directed, and starred in their revues at the New Yorker. The ice-skaters were provided with musical accompaniment from

Century Room, Hotel Adolphus,

popular bands. Diners at the Terrace Room sipped their cocktails and viewed a spectacle of beautifully costumed performers gliding across the ice in a tantalizing array of figure-skating feats. After the performance, the ice rink retracted under the orchestra allowing patrons to dance to the sounds of bands such as Woody Herman, Benny Goodman, and Gus Arnheim.

The supper club ice-skating shows remained a craze from the mid-1930s, 1940s, and 1950s. In homage to the spectacular and sparkling ice shows, we present two cocktails specially created by renowned mixologist Jim Hewes of the Round Robin Bar in Washington DC's historic Willard Hotel.

👉 Thin Ice Cocktail

2 ounces dry gin
½ ounce Bénédictine
1 sugar cube
2–3 dashes Absinthe

1–2 dashes Peychaud's bitters
Dry champagne
Lemon twist, for garnish

Mix dry gin and Bénédictine over ice. Soak sugar cube with absinthe and Peychaud's bitters and place the sugar cube in a champagne flute. Fill one-third of the champagne flute with shaved ice. Strain the gin mixture into the champagne flute and top with champagne. Garnish with a lemon twist.

Sonja's Sun Valley Sunrise

2 ounces silver tequila
½ ounce triple sec
¼ ounce agave nectar
1 ounce pineapple juice
1 ounce fresh orange juice

1 ounce fresh lime juice
¼ ounce Chambord
¼ ounce pomegranate juice
Mint sprig, for garnish
Orange wheel, for garnish

Place all ingredients, except the Chambord and pomegranate juice, in a cocktail shaker filled with ice and shake. Pour the Chambord and pomegranate juice into a wine goblet and fill halfway with crushed ice. Pour the shaken ingredients into the wine goblet and garnish with a sprig of mint and orange wheel.

BOULEVARD ROOM

THE STEVENS • CHICAGO

A HILTON HOTEL

Southwest

H-4452   THE WATCHTOWER AT DESERT VIEW, GRAND CANYON NATIONAL PARK, ARIZONA

Fred Harvey Southwestern Special

Fred Harvey, a pioneer in the hospitality industry, had a profound effect on American culture. Arriving in the United States in 1853, Harvey was destined to create a chain of restaurants and hotels alongside newly established railways. As a recipient of poor-quality food and accommodations during rail travel, Harvey sought to make improvements in trackside service. In 1876, Harvey entered an agreement with the fledgling Atchison, Topeka, and Santa Fe Railway (AT&SF) to provide quality meals and comfortable accommodations to weary travelers.

To obtain quality waitstaff at his restaurants, Harvey employed "single, well-mannered females of character and intelligence" providing them with room, board, and a monthly salary. The "Harvey Girls," known for their official uniform of starched black dress and white apron, provided a genteel element to the "Wild West."

Although Harvey died in 1901, his family carried on the company that became famous for its style, service, and quality. The innovative architect, Mary Jane Colter, worked for the company from 1902 to 1948. Her distinctive designs used a combination of Craftsman, Spanish, Native American, and Mexican elements. Colter's Southwestern style is noted in such Harvey creations as the Desert View Watchtower (1932), an observation structure located at the Grand Canyon, Arizona; La Posada Hotel (1929) in Winslow, Arizona; and La Fonda Hotel (1922) in Santa Fe, New Mexico. Completing the Southwestern experience, Native Americans were hired to craft jewelry, blankets, and artifacts, which were sold as souvenirs in Harvey Company gift shops.

A genius at branding, Harvey incorporated elements of the environment and the ethnicity of local residents to create a

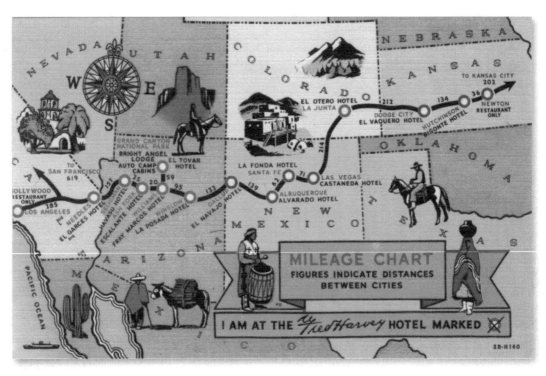

satisfying experience for travelers. This philosophy is reflected in the recipe provided by the Fred Harvey Company in Ted Saucier's 1951 book, *Bottoms Up*. The Fred Harvey Southwestern Special is a pleasing mixture of Spanish and Mexican ingredients, offering a regionally inspired cocktail. Climb aboard and enjoy a taste of Fred Harvey and the old Southwest.

☞ Fred Harvey Southwestern Special

1 ounce Spanish brandy
½ ounce Kahlúa
Splash of Anís del Mono liqueur

Place all the ingredients in a cocktail shaker with cracked ice, shake, and strain into a cocktail glass.

✳ *Note: The original recipe calls for a splash of Ojen, which is no longer produced. Anís del Mono is a good substitute, but any anise-flavored liqueur will do.*

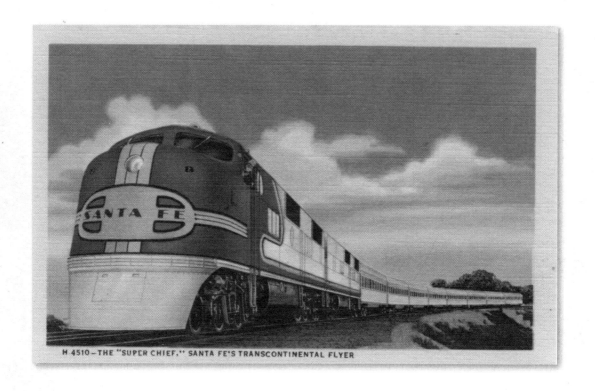

H 4510—THE "SUPER CHIEF," SANTA FE'S TRANSCONTINENTAL FLYER

Santa Fe Cooler

The Atchison, Topeka, and Santa Fe (AT&SF) Railway initially connected Atchison and Topeka, Kansas, with Santa Fe, New Mexico. Through growth and acquisition, it developed into a major force, providing rail service west to California, east to Illinois, and south through Texas into Louisiana. At its peak, the AT&SF owned more than 13,000 miles of track.

One of the most famous trains on the AT&SF line was the legendary *Super Chief.* Making its initial run from Dearborn Station in Chicago, Illinois, on May 12, 1936, the diesel-powered passenger train arrived in Los Angeles, California, in less than 40 hours. The re-launch in 1937, with improved tracks and lighter stock, reduced the trip to 37 hours. Bearing a distinctive red and yellow paint scheme on its locomotive, the *Super Chief* was known as "the train of the stars." Celebrities traveling to Hollywood could connect in Chicago and take the *Super Chief* to Los Angeles.

H-4512—LOUNGE CAR ON THE SANTA FE'S "SUPER CHIEF"

H-4511—ONE OF THE DINING CARS ON THE SANTA FE'S "SUPER CHIEF"

H-1885   THE ESCALANTE, FRED HARVEY HOTEL, ASH FORK, ARIZONA

During the 1940s, promotion of the AT&SF fell under the domain of the company's public relations manager, Lee Lyles. It was Lyles who arranged for celebrities to be photographed on board the *Super Chief* as proof of the train's importance and prestige. An article in the *Atchison Daily Globe*, on March 16, 1945, credited Lyles for suggesting a magazine story about the Fred Harvey system along the AT&SF line. The story developed into the 1946 MGM musical film, *The Harvey Girls*, starring Judy Garland and featuring the Warren–Mercer hit song "On the Atchison, Topeka, and Santa Fe." The film and popular song were worth an unfathomable amount of advertising for the AT&SF.

In 1946, Lyles met with author Ayn Rand to discuss features of management and operations at the AT&SF for her book, *Atlas Shrugged*. The research questions she prepared for Lyles were later published in *The Journals of Ayn Rand* and provided accurate characterization for the fictional railroad executives in her book.

A competent public relations man, Lyles was also capable of mixing a drink. The Santa Fe Cooler, credited to Lyles, is a sumptuous combination of Applejack, curaçao, lime juice, Cointreau, and champagne, reminiscent of the golden age of train travel.

Santa Fe Cooler

1½ ounces of Applejack
½ ounce curaçao
½ ounce Cointreau
Juice of 1 lime
Dry Champagne

Place the Applejack, curaçao, Cointreau, and lime juice in a cocktail shaker. Shake well and pour into a tall glass. Add cracked ice and fill glass with champagne.

Tequila Sunrise

The Arizona Biltmore Hotel in Phoenix, crowned the "Jewel of the Desert," opened in February 1929. The Biltmore's architectural design was influenced by Frank Lloyd Wright and set on thirty-nine acres in the desert against the backdrop of Squaw Peak. For the first 40 years, the hotel was open to well-heeled guests by invitation only.

Prohibition did not stop the hotel from providing cocktails to their out-of-town guests. The reading room by day/smoking room by night was actually a speakeasy in which guests and bootleg whiskey were brought up through a set of secret stairs from the kitchen. Hotel guests only had to purchase the glasses, ice, and mixers; the alcohol was provided "free of charge."

The Catalina Pool, a beautiful Art Deco–tiled masterpiece, was a favorite of guests, particularly Marilyn Monroe, who stated that it was her favorite pool in the whole world.

808 A DESERT SUNSET.

9-2111

p-73   Swimming Pool and Cabanas, with P. K. Wrigley Residence

and Arizona Biltmore Hotel in Background   1C-H1031

Purportedly, Irving Berlin wrote the tune, "A White Christmas," while sitting poolside. Another guest who enjoyed sunbathing and drinking at the pool approached Biltmore's bartender, Gene Sulit, and asked him to create a "surprise" cocktail using tequila. Sulit presented the Tequila Sunrise, a two-toned potion in which the denser ingredient, the cassis, settles on the bottom of the glass, while the lighter ingredients rise to the top, mimicking a sunrise.

Cocktail aficionados might be more familiar with the modern version of the Sunrise that uses orange juice and grenadine. Step back in time and try the original Biltmore recipe!

☞ Tequila Sunrise

1¼ ounces tequila
¾ ounce crème de cassis
Fresh lime
Soda water
Orange wheel, for garnish

Fill glass with cracked ice. Add tequila, crème de cassis, and a squeeze of lime. Fill with soda. Garnish with fresh orange wheel.

307—International Bridge Connecting El Paso, Texas and Juarez, Old Mexico

Conga Cooler

The Conga Cooler was one of the many potions created by head barman Pancho Morales at Tommy's Place in Ciudad Juárez, Mexico, in the early 1940s. Signs over the bar advertised drinks to "Hemingway types" and soldiers who were living in the moment. Morales claims to have created the Margarita, and other interesting concoctions such as the "P-38" and "B-29" named after World War II military aircrafts. The Conga Cooler was by far the most popular drink at Tommy's. It was touted as "famous and original with refreshing qualities and a long remembered taste," in the local papers.

Tommy's was one of the many nightspots that clustered around the Santa Fe Bridge connecting Ciudad Juárez and El Paso, Texas. The two cities shared economic, cultural, and ethnic bonds and benefited from each other's proximity. An aggressive marketing campaign encouraged travelers, businesses, and homebuyers throughout the United States to discover El Paso.

PROFESSOR VALLES AND HIS FAMOUS MEXICAN TIPICA ORCHESTRA, EL PASO, TEXAS 19

J-6—Juarez Avenue by Night, Juarez, Old Mexico

One could enjoy the amenities of a modern American city, and at the same time partake in the pleasures of Mexico just minutes across the bridge. Old-world charm, a foreign atmosphere, and legal drinking and gambling were guaranteed. El Paso was also an important tourist stop for adventure seekers on their way to and from Carlsbad Caverns in New Mexico.

The city of Juárez benefited from Americans' penchant for good fun, food, and drink. Tourists had no difficulty filling their vacation calendars to enjoy Mexi-

can bullfights and horse racing. Restaurants and bars advertised businessmen's lunches, quality dining, top-shelf alcohol, and refined entertainment in the evenings. While some floorshows included magicians and comedians, most included American or European orchestras alternating blues, jazz, or dance music of the tango or Charleston. "Mexican Tipica" orchestras

J-4—Lobby No. 2 Cafe and Night Club, Juárez, Old Mexico

TX-7 THE DANCE OF THE "SOMBRERO"

7A-H1305

© C. T. & CO.

performed traditional music in regional costume. The Lis Follies claimed their entertainment was "peppy and will keep one keyed up from the start to the finish!"

American soldiers from nearby Fort Bliss were welcomed at Tommy's Place to enjoy the air-cooled comfort, home-cooked meals, and good fellowship. With so many drink choices at the bar, it's no wonder that Tommy's was a popular respite for the military patrons.

Conga Cooler

2 ounces silver tequila
½ ounce pineapple juice
3 dashes Angostura bitters
3 ounces chilled club soda
Lemon peel, for garnish

Pour all ingredients, except club soda, into an Old Fashioned glass and stir. Fill with large ice cubes and top with soda. Stir again. Add lemon peel garnish.

Atomic Cocktail

From 1951 to 1962, Las Vegas, Nevada, was the epicenter for a propaganda and marketing blitz that spread across the country, glorifying the atomic bomb. The US Department of Energy began experimenting with bombs in a nuclear testing site sixty-five miles outside the city. The hospitality industry jumped on the bandwagon by providing opportunities for patrons and residents to view the atomic blasts at hotels, restaurants, and bar rooftops.

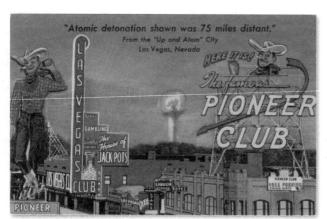

The Chamber of Commerce and casino operators such as Benny Binion of the Horseshoe Club provided calendars and postcards with dates, times, and best vantage points to view the explosions. A prime example is the best-selling postcard of "Vegas Vic," the forty-foot-tall cowboy that welcomed tourists to Las Vegas as an Old West–style town, while an atomic cloud hung in the air. There was clearly an interdependent relationship between the nuclear and tourist industry.

Atomic themes flourished in Vegas, from parades to hairstyles. Beauty pageants featured contestants wearing the "atomic hairdo," created by Gee Gee, a hairstylist at the Flamingo Hotel, in which hair was pulled over a mushroom-shaped wire frame, and sprinkled with silver glitter. Atomic Liquors, named after the nearby explosions, was established in 1952 as the first and now oldest freestanding bar in Las Vegas. In those early days, celebrities, looking to get away from their fans, enjoyed the camaraderie of this establishment and its pool table.

Perhaps guests at the Flamingo Hotel and other establishments on the strip celebrated the atomic blasts with the sparkly and "toxic" Atomic Cocktail, while enjoying the hip jazz notes of Slim Gaillard Quartette's satirical song with the same name.

 # Atomic Cocktail

1½ ounces vodka
1½ ounces brandy
1 teaspoon sherry
1½ ounces dry champagne

Stir the vodka, brandy, and sherry with cracked ice. Strain into a chilled cocktail glass and add champagne.

Moscow Mule

Throwing your ring in the Truckee River and going for the "Reno cure" were popular euphemisms for a quick divorce. Tens of thousands of divorce seekers traveled to Nevada after the State Legislature legalized gambling and liberal divorce laws in 1931. Restaurants, gambling halls, and hotels outdid each other with lavish furnishings, flamboyant entertainment, and distinctive gambling games capturing the divorce trade.

The El Cortez Hotel was one of the first to cater to the divorce-bound. Built in 1931, this six-story Art Deco–style hotel was the tallest building in Reno. Its elegant Trocadero Club was designed with floating walls and ceilings and modern indirect fluorescent lighting. Mirrors created an optical illusion behind the sixty-foot leather upholstered bar with slot machines placed prominently around the room. Donald Macky, architect of the Elephant Towers at the 1939 Golden Gate International Exposition, designed stylized wall murals of

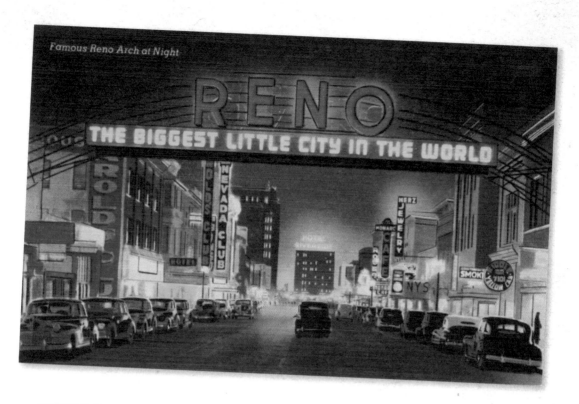

Famous Reno Arch at Night

RENO
THE BIGGEST LITTLE CITY IN THE WORLD

The Golden Girls
Complete Floor Shows Nitely

dancers. Top performers such as the Andrew Sisters and Victor Borge entertained patrons.

Smaller establishments also enjoyed Reno's tourist largesse. The Piccadilly Bar was styled like an old English pub. A tongue-in-cheek sentiment figured above the bar: "Dear Souls—from these kindly goblets take a sip—t'will curl thy pensive tear—tis not as sweet as woman's lips, but ah 'tis more sincere." In 1947, patrons enjoyed the Moscow Mule, an exclusive feature of the bar. An announcement in the *Reno Gazette* exclaimed that the "MOSCOW MULE now comes to Reno!" Originating from Hollywood's English-styled Cock 'N Bull tavern, the Mule was served in twelve-ounce copper mugs engraved with an image of a kicking mule and displayed on pegs above the back bar.

It was Jack Morgan, owner of the Cock 'N Bull, and his buddy John Martin, president of Heublein & Sons, who purportedly created the Moscow Mule. Martin had purchased the vodka formula from Smirnoff in 1939 and Morgan had a large inventory of imported peppery ginger beer. The twosome combined

Giant Ceramic Mural, Fabulous Harold's Club, Reno, Nevada

9B-H1729

9A-H1147

the vodka and beer and marketed it in a copper mug. Martin traveled around the country introducing the concoction to the tavern trade. Martin took two photos with his Polaroid camera of the bartender holding a mug and a bottle of vodka. One photo remained at the bar; the second was placed in an album and brought to the next tavern showing how the competition was already serving the drink. This may be how the Mule came to the Piccadilly and other establishments in Reno. Advertisements incongruously described the Mule as insidious, hair-raising, and a "mellow masterpiece." Try the Moscow Mule and describe it for yourself!

 # Moscow Mule

Juice of ½ lime
2 ounces vodka
Ginger beer
Lime slice, for garnish

Squeeze the lime into a copper mug, rocks, or Collins glass. Drop the lime into the mug. Fill with ice cubes and add the vodka. Add ginger beer and garnish with a lime slice.

Trends from the mid-1930s–50s:

Tropical Paradise

From the 1930s onward, an awareness and embrace of Pacific Islands culture grabbed hold of the American psyche through radio, music, dance, and film. The radio show, *Hawaii Calls*, enthralled American listeners with live Hawaiian music broadcast each week, starting in 1935 from the courtyard of the Moana Hotel on Waikiki Beach. Bing Crosby's 1937 film, *Waikiki Wedding*, rhapsodized melodically about the Hawaiian Islands.

The 1939 Golden Gate International Exposition recognized and celebrated "A Pageant of the Pacific," an homage to the Pacific Islands. A 392-foot Tower of the Sun and an

THE ONLY AUTHENTIC CUBAN-SPANISH RESTAURANT IN AMERICA

BLUE MIRROR — "A TROPICAL ATMOSPHERE OF REFINEMENT"

275 CLINTON AVE. — NEWARK, NEW JERSEY   6A-H2169

eighty-foot statue of Pacifica, goddess of the Pacific Ocean, welcomed visitors to the fair, inviting them to enjoy the traditional arts of Southeast countries and islands. President Franklin D. Roosevelt stressed harmony and unity of the Pacific nations with the United States. American servicemen returning home from World War II brought memories and keepsakes of their time in the Pacific. *Tales of the South Pacific*, James Michener's 1948 collection of short stories, which served as the basis for the Rodgers and Hammerstein musical *South Pacific*, generated American interest in these distant lands.

It is not surprising that the restaurant and entertainment industry jumped on the bandwagon, luring patrons to bask in the glow of a faux-tropical utopia. What could beat an

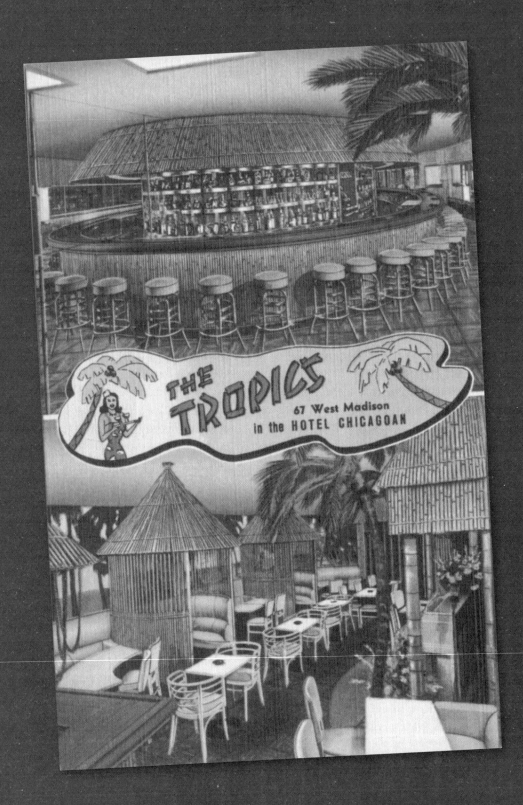

THE TROPICS

67 West Madison
in the HOTEL CHICAGOAN

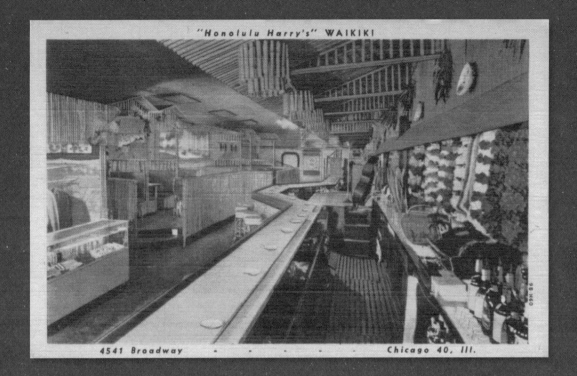

"Honolulu Harry's" WAIKIKI

4541 Broadway · · · · · Chicago 40, Ill.

evening in paradise? Palm branches swaying in a gentle breeze, raindrops drumming against a tin roof, and lei-bedecked revelers enjoying exotic cocktails . . .

Don Beach was one of the first in a line of entrepreneurs to create an exotic getaway for the stay-up-lates. Don, a bootlegger during prohibition, decorated a small shop in Hollywood in 1933 with souvenirs from his travels in the Caribbean and South Pacific. He served novel tasting Cantonese–style dishes to the Hollywood set, alongside rum concoctions with tropical fruits and juices such as the Zombie and Three Dots and a Dash. Female guests were given leis and water was sprayed on the tin roof to simulate a tropical rainstorm.

Trader Vic's South Seas-inspired establishments were so successful that the owner,

Victor Bergeron, opened a chain of restaurants worldwide. Trader Vic's served exotic food and distinctive cocktails such as the Kava Bowl, an orchid festooned rum and fruit concoction.

Large venues such as the Palm Bar and its adjacent Starlight Roof at the Waldorf–Astoria in New York and the Cocoanut Grove at the Ambassador Hotel in California also utilized strong designs to imaginative tropical effects with artistic scenes of foliage, flamingos, monkeys, palm trees, and canvas canopies. Restaurateurs from Maine to Alaska followed this popular trend, decorating supper clubs, lounges, and restaurants with bamboo and rattan furniture, thatched-roof bars and dining alcoves, palm trees, murals of volcanoes and Island life, and exotic birds.

Hollywood's bar and restaurant scene was home to a multitude of Hawaiin-inspired drinking locales such as King's Tropical Inn, Ken's Hula Hut, and the Seven Seas. Clifton's Pacific Seas dining establishment, while not a nightclub, exemplified the spirit of Polynesian paradise. The exterior was constructed of faux stones, waterfalls, and exotic plants. Quiet organ music greeted the diners amid gorgeous tropical foliage, an aviary, a volcano, a meditation garden, and fifteen- to twenty-foot neon-lit flowers. Hawaiian entertainers graced the bamboo stage and waiters sang the menu. From 1931 until it closed thirty years later, Clifton's restaurant practiced the "Golden Rule" and provided free or penny meals to over a million homeless and hungry people.

Known as the "informal cocktail lounge and dining room of the motion picture industry," Harry Sugarman's Sugie's Hollywood Tropics was frequented by both celebrities and paparazzi. Sugie, as Harry became known, managed the day-to-day operations of the Grauman Theater and was notorious for throwing lavish events at the opening of a new film. His first restaurant was located across the street from the theater. Filipino bartenders created drinks named after starlets whose photo portraits were emblazoned around a gold star on the menu. Sugie would later use this idea to help conceive the Hollywood Walk of Fame. A second location on Vine and Sunset was home to a number of fashion shows and was constantly the talk of the town—the gossip columnists spotted dining twosomes from the Hollywood jet set.

Climbing up the faux gangplank to the *S.S. Aloha*, guests were greeted at Honolulu Harry's Club Waikiki in Chicago with authentic music and dancing by Hawaiian and Tahitian performers. In 1943, Harry Nakamura's first club in Chicago, Playtime, was an informal "headquarters" to the GIs that served in the 100th and 442nd Infantry Battalions. Harry had spent two and a half years during the war in an internment camp in Utah and moved to Chicago when the war was over. Playtime provided a place for his fellow Hawaiian-Japanese-Americans that had served in the war. In 1946, Harry moved to new quarters, continuing his policy of hiring only authentic Hawaiian talent. The souvenir shop sold aloha shirts with bold patterns and color. The combination of Chinese, Japanese, Hawaiian, and American cuisine, hula lessons, leis for the ladies, luau nights, and exotic island cocktails made Club Waikiki a true escape to paradise.

Tropical-themed restaurants and nightclubs dotted the country, transplanting guests to another continent away from the hustle and bustle of their everyday realities. A frenzy of palm trees and rum drinks, coupled with Hawaiian dancers and ukulele players, set the stage for fun-seekers in this era. By the 1950s, the tropical theme morphed into a new American aesthetic inspired by Polynesian carvings and mythology. All manner of businesses jumped on the Tiki bandwagon.

Entrepreneurs created a fantasy world using natural materials from the tropics, totems, and flotsam and jetsam. Americans flocked to restaurants, bowling alleys, and hotels that adopted the South Seas elements. Who wouldn't want to spend an evening enjoying exotic food and drink in a place such as the Cannibal Cocktail Lounge?

Enjoy a cocktail created by Lucinda Sterling of Middle Branch and Seaborne Bars in New York City, and hark back to a time when the Pacific Island images were fresh in the minds of Americans.

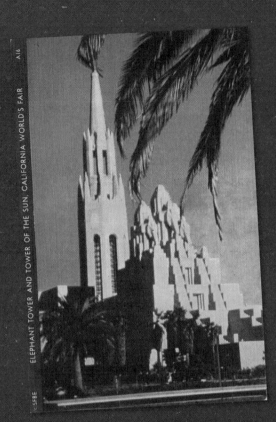

ELEPHANT TOWER AND TOWER OF THE SUN, CALIFORNIA WORLD'S FAIR

 Playtime Punch

1 ounce spiced rum
1 ounce blended scotch
½ ounce triple sec
¾ ounce fresh lime juice
½ ounce pineapple juice

¼ ounce grenadine
1 ounce club soda or seltzer
Pineapple slice or lime wedge, for garnish

Combine all ingredients, except soda, into a cocktail shaker or mixing glass. Add ice to the shaker, and shake ingredients with ice about three to four times, then strain into a highball glass over ice. Top with club soda or seltzer. Garnish with a slice of pineapple or lime wedge.

LA-90   AMBASSADOR HOTEL, LOS ANGELES, CALIFORNIA

Cocoanut Grove Cocktail

The Cocoanut Grove Cocktail bears the name of its world-class nightclub and restaurant, located at the Ambassador Hotel in Los Angeles, California. The grand opening of the hotel in 1921 ushered in more than six decades of culture, entertainment, and history making.

The Cocoanut Grove was a favorite meeting place for Hollywood celebrities, US presidents from Hoover to Nixon, royalty, and the hoi polloi. The list of entertainers, guests, and residents at the Ambassador is endless. Mary Pickford, Douglas Fairbanks, Lucy and Desi Arnaz, Jack Dempsey, and Judy Garland were just a few famous people who took a bow or enjoyed an evening's entertainment there. Lena Horne, a celebrated entertainer and civil rights activist, was the first African American to stay as a guest after headlining at the Grove. The Cocoanut

The World Famous Cocoanut Grove · Los Angeles Ambassador

"WORLD FAMOUS COCOANUT GROVE" AT THE AMBASSADOR HOTEL, LOS ANGELES, CALIFORNIA

Grove was home to six Academy Award ceremonies between 1930 and 1943. In the 1940 ceremony with Bob Hope as the emcee, the Academy bestowed thirteen awards to the film, *Gone with the Wind*.

Architect Julius Ralph Davidson designed the Ambassador's centerpiece nightclub in 1926 and used his experience as a set designer for renowned MGM's art director Cedric Gibbons and film director Cecil B. DeMille. Davidson employed lavish Mediterranean and Moorish decorative patterns throughout the club in arches, tiles, filigree chandeliers, and gold-leaf trimmings. Original props from Rudolph Valentino's 1921 film, *The Sheik*, such as the papier-mâché palm trees and mechanical monkeys with amber-lit eyes, enhanced the decor. A real waterfall added a thrilling vibe to this glamorous "playground of the stars." The room's wide staircase created a grand entrance for celebrities and guests especially during the Academy Awards presentation.

The origins of the Cocoanut Grove Cocktail remain a mystery. Exotic ingredients in this drink added to the delight of those seeking a fun evening at the Ambassador Hotel's glamorous nightspot.

Cocoanut Grove Cocktail

2½ ounces white Puerto Rican rum
½ ounce orange curaçao
1 ounce lime juice
½ ounce coconut cream

Put everything in a blender with 1 cup crushed ice and blend for 30 seconds or until smooth. Pour into a cocktail glass.

Brown Derby Cocktail

The Golden Age of Hollywood flourished in the 1930s. Following the stock market crash of 1929 and the first successful talking picture, *The Jazz Singer* (1927), the movie industry reached a crucial turning point. The combination of voiced film features, glamorous new stars, and elaborate movie sets provided welcome escapism, and helped carry the American public through the trying years of the Great Depression.

Billy Wilkerson was among the movers and shakers who found their way to Hollywood seeking fame and fortune. Wilkerson established the *Hollywood Reporter* in 1930 and owned several popular nightclubs such as the Vendome Club (1933), Café Trocadero (1934), and Ciro's (1940). A galaxy of stars frequented his venues, providing continuous fodder for his entertainment industry newspaper. It was at the Vendome Club that the Brown Derby Cocktail was first served. To this day, no one knows why Wilkerson named his cocktail after a rival restaurant.

There were four Brown Derby restaurants that opened in Los Angeles between 1926 and 1940, but the Hollywood Brown Derby was the most famous. The restaurant was a short distance from film and radio studios, and supplied a steady stream of celebrity customers. Owner Bill Cobb, creator of the Cobb salad, maintained a hospitable atmosphere for his star-studded clientele. Carole Lombard and Clark Gable were reportedly engaged there, while comedian Jack Benny and his wife, Mary, sat in a booth and worked on their scripts. Regulars included Vivien Leigh, Laurence Olivier, Tyrone Power, Marlene Dietrich, gossip columnist Louella Parsons, as well as Hollywood's most important producers, directors, and agents.

The Hollywood Brown Derby was known for its caricatures. The tradition began in 1931 when an artist named Eddie Vitch offered to sketch portraits of famous diners in exchange for a

847—Hollywood Boulevard at Night, Hollywood, California

0B-H1932

843—The Rendezvous of the Stars, The Brown Derby, Hollywood, California

THE BROWN DERBY RESTAURANT, — 1628 N. VINE ST., — HOLLYWOOD, CALIF.

meal. The drawings were signed by the celebrity and placed on the restaurant's "Great Wall of Fame." Having your picture displayed at the Brown Derby was a symbol of status, and diners enjoyed spotting the likeness of their favorite stars.

The Brown Derby Cocktail's warm and bright flavors harken back to the days of old-time Hollywood when it was possible for ordinary people to mingle with the rich, the powerful, and the famous.

☞ Brown Derby Cocktail

2 ounces bourbon
1 ounce fresh grapefruit juice
½ ounce honey syrup
(mix 1 part honey to 1 part water, warm in a saucepan until dissolved, cool before use)

Shake all ingredients in a cocktail shaker filled with ice and strain into a chilled cocktail glass.

801—Earl Carroll Theatre-Restaurant, Hollywood, California

MacArthur Cocktail

The sentimental ballad, "Cocktails for Two," features a couple enjoying cocktails at a romantic rendezvous. This was the first drinking song produced at the end of Prohibition. "Cocktails for Two" was featured in Paramount's 1934 hit film, *Murder at the Vanities*. The film was based on Earl Carroll's lavish musical extravaganzas at the Earl Carroll Theater in New York that ran from 1922 to 1932. The productions featured scantily clad showgirls who met Carroll's exacting standards: 5'5" tall, 118 pounds with a list of specific body measurements. Ironically, his "Ten Demandments of Beauty" expected that the dancers extolled virtuous behavior, grace, and dignity.

In 1938, Carroll built the largest entertainment hall in the world on Sunset Boulevard in Hollywood, combining the best features of a nightclub, restaurant, and theater. The building's

Streamline Moderne style incorporated walls of mirrors with etched-glass murals, voluptuous statues, a tear-drop–shaped theater, a grand staircase flanked by brass handrails, fluted columns made of glass and pastel-hued fluorescent tubing. The theater had a seating capacity of 1,000 and included two revolving stages where almost bare dancers entertained Hollywood celebrities and tourists.

The façade of the building featured the "Wall of Fame," which consisted of 125 autographed cement blocks by luminaries such as Cary Grant, Clark Gable, and Shirley Temple. A twenty-foot tall neon image of Carroll's leading lady, Beryl Wallace, and the motto THE MOST BEAUTIFUL GIRLS IN THE WORLD adorned the entranceway. Wallace performed as the star entertainer in the old and new Earl Carroll theaters and acted in a variety of movies. Carroll and Wallace's relationship was both professional and deeply romantic.

Carroll and Wallace were close friends with the celebrated World War II hero General Douglas MacArthur. The couple visited MacArthur in various places around the world, including

Write your impressions of the Theatre on reverse side. . . Give to Waiter. We will pay postage.

(THIS SIDE OF CARD FOR ADDRESS ONLY)

BERYL WALLACE
EARL CARROLL THEATRE-RESTAURANT
The Glamour Spot of Glamorous Hollywood..!

West Point while he was Superintendent and in Tokyo in the 1940s. In a letter to MacArthur dated March 1948, Carroll reminded his friend that the American people idolized him. Carroll applauded MacArthur's good humor and sense of true values, and recommended keeping up this demeanor until his nomination for President of the United States. Sadly, Carroll and Wallace died when their plane crashed en route to the MacArthur-for-President Headquarters at the Republican Convention in June 1948. It seems fitting to remember these prominent entertainers with a drink created in honor of their dear friend, Douglas MacArthur.

☛ MacArthur Cocktail

2 ounces white rum
½ ounce triple sec
Juice of ½ lime
3 dashes Jamaican rum
1 dash egg white

Shake with ice in a cocktail shaker and strain into a chilled glass.

853—The "Wall of Fame", Earl Carroll's Theatre-Restaurant, Hollywood, California

Del Monte
Lodge Cocktail

In 1880, railroad tycoon Charles Crocker constructed a
vast seaside resort conceptualized as a playground for the
rich in Monterey, California. Crocker was one of the "Big
Four" owners of the Central and Southern Pacific Railways
and laid tracks to transport guests to his 20,000-acre property. The Hotel Del Monte was the centerpiece of the resort,
which included gardens, hunting, swimming, horseback
riding, and a scenic seventeen-mile drive along the coast to
entertain his guests.

The once popular resort began to fall on hard times at the
beginning of the twentieth century. In 1915, Hotel Del Monte
and its parent corporation, the Pacific Improvement Company,
hired Samuel F. B. Morse to revitalize the property. Morse, a
former quarterback at Yale University, envisioned the resort as

a center for sports, offering golf, polo, horse racing, deep-sea fishing, and yachting.

Under Morse's guidance, the Del Monte Lodge and the Pebble Beach Golf Links opened in 1919. Morse purchased the Pacific Improvement Company with financial backing and renamed it Del Monte Properties. The area became known as Pebble Beach. One of his dreams was to host the US Open at Pebble Beach Golf Links, which became a reality.

During World War II, the Navy took up residence at the Hotel Del Monte. Morse sold the Hotel Del Monte and part of the property in 1947 to the US Naval Academy, which eventually housed its Naval Postgraduate School.

Many celebrity golfers have enjoyed the favorable climate at Pebble Beach. In 1947, singer, actor, and avid golfer Bing Crosby began hosting his National Pro-Am Tournament at Pebble Beach Golf Links and the surrounding golf courses. Bing loved the course and credited Morse with his foresight, stating, "I shall always be grateful to that eminent sportsman

Sam Morse, the man whose vision, dedication, and devotion to quality made this one of the showplaces of the world."

Both the Del Monte Lodge, now known as the Lodge at Pebble Beach, and the Pebble Beach Golf Links continue to provide grand style and luxury to its visitors. The Del Monte Lodge Cocktail bears a resemblance to the Brandy Alexander but the substitution of Kahlúa is an enjoyable variation.

☞ Del Monte Lodge Cocktail

1½ ounces Kahlúa
1½ ounces brandy
1½ ounces half-and-half cream

Place all ingredients in a cocktail shaker filled with ice and shake vigorously, and strain into a chilled cocktail glass.

M13   DEL MONTE LODGE, NEAR MONTEREY, CALIFORNIA

MARKET ST. LOOKING EAST FROM POWELL ST., SAN FRANCISCO, CALIF.   5

© STANLEY A. PILTZ   8A-H2819

Sir Francis Drake Special

It's late at night. You hear the clanging bell of a San Francisco cable car outside on the street. You are alone in your hotel room. You have no ice. What do you do? Concoct this Scaffa-style drink served at room temperature! The Sir Francis Drake Special originally appeared in Ted Saucier's *Bottoms Up* cocktail compilation (1951). Aromatic and strong ingredients characterize the Scaffa-style drink, which typically includes liquor, one or two liqueurs, and an occasional dash of bitters. Stirred without ice to dilute it, this drink is sure to banish your worries and make all right with the world.

The Sir Francis Drake Hotel, namesake of the drink, was built in San Francisco, California, in 1928 during the height of Prohibition. State of the art, the hotel offered every modern convenience. One of these features was the Servidor, which allowed items to be placed in a compartment through the guest room doors. A handy feature during Prohibition, the Servidor permitted the discrete delivery of alcohol to be enjoyed in the privacy of one's room. The hotel was equipped with a hidden room between the lobby and the mezzanine level where alcohol was stored. Illegal liquor smuggled into nearby San Mateo from Canada was delivered to the hotel's basement, where a special elevator transported the booze inconspicuously to the hidden room. This ensured that guests staying at "The Drake" were truly afforded every luxury. Following the repeal of Prohibition, the hotel's Persian Room and rooftop Starlite Lounge provided guests atmospheric venues to imbibe legally once more.

☞ Sir Francis Drake Special

½ ounce gin
½ ounce bonded rye whiskey
½ ounce triple sec (or Cointreau)
½ ounce Green Chartreuse

Stir without ice and serve in a glass.

✳ *Note: Bonded rye is not necessary—any rye whiskey will do.*

Chinatown Cocktail

Step onto Grant Avenue in San Francisco's Chinatown and you will be transported to a faraway, exotic, oriental-themed fantasy. Red awnings, pagoda-style roofs, lantern-shaped streetlights, and brightly colored signs all strategically arranged to create an American version of Chinese culture. Following the devastating earthquake of 1906, much of the city was destroyed and Chinatown was slated for relocation. Merchants resisted the move and created a new image for the district allowing reconstruction of Chinatown to remain in the same area.

Tourists flocked to the new Chinatown with its herbal shops, dragon parades, Chinese bazaars, and theatrical chinoiserie. In the evening, glowing neon signs beckoned hungry visitors into chop suey palaces with names such as Shanghai Low, Cathay House, and Lotus Bowl. Following the repeal of Prohibition, Chinese nightclubs opened, adding another level of entertainment to the bustling neighborhood. Chinese performers that were unable to break into Hollywood found a niche in the shows at nightclubs such as Forbidden City, Chinese Skyroom, and Kubla Kahn. Here, one might find Humphrey Bogart, Ronald Reagan, or Duke Ellington out on the town enjoying the performance. During the 1940s, the nightclubs became a destination for soldiers passing through San Francisco on their way to the Pacific.

Club Shanghai was one of the popular nightclubs located on Chinatown's Grant Avenue. D. W. Low, owner of Shanghai Low restaurant and Club Shanghai, advertised his nightclub as "a smart cocktail bar, with music, dancing and floorshow nightly, where excellent Chinese food can be enjoyed." Exotic-sounding cocktails and liquors were listed on the menu such as Shanghai Sling, Shanghai Special, Ng Gar Pai, and Mui Kwe Lu.

Later, Club Shanghai was sold to herbalist Fong Wan. An astute businessman, Fong Wan owned venues in Chinatown, as well as nearby Oakland. His revues at Club Shanghai were advertised to "import outstanding acts from China" and included singers, dancers, acrobats, and comedians. The nightclubs were a steppingstone for many Chinese-American actors striving for a career in film or television. Chinese-American entertainer, Sammee Tong, was a master of ceremonies at Fong Wan's Club Shanghai. Tong went on to star as a wise-cracking "houseboy" in the television show, *Bachelor Father*, which debuted in 1957. Chinatown's night-club scene was so fascinating, Rogers and Hammerstein based their 1958 play, *Flower Drum Song*, on the setting. The Chinatown Cocktail appeared in the book, *Hollywood Cocktails* (1933).

SAMMEE TONG'S REVUE AT FONG WAN'S CLUB SHANGHAI, CHINATOWN, SAN FRANCISCO

GRANT AVENUE, CHINATOWN, SAN FRANCISCO, CALIF. 63

 Chinatown Cocktail

1 ounce gin
1 ounce Italian vermouth (sweet)
1 ounce French vermouth (dry)
1 dash brandy
1 dash lemon or lime juice
1 dash orange bitters
Lemon twist, for garnish

Shake all with ice in a cocktail shaker and strain into a
chilled cocktail glass. Garnish with lemon peel twist.

Technology and the Cocktail Bar:

Bowling Lane Lounges from the 1940s–50s

The 1950s ushered in a new era of consumer spending and entertainment. For the first time, bowling centers across the country provided fun and sport for all ages and social classes due to modern technologies in pinsetting and television broadcasting.

It was the automation of the pinsetter in 1952, first introduced by Brunswick Corporation and refined for popular use by AMF Bowling Centers, that changed the future of bowling. Before the automation of pinsetting, bowling alley proprietors hired young boys and men called

835—Vine Street, Looking North from Sunset Boulevard, Hollywood, California

OB-H391

SUNSET BOWLING CENTER — Home of the famous 52 Lanes in a Row

PLAYERS	FIRST GAME										NET TOTAL	SECOND GAME										NET TOTAL	THIRD GAME										NET TOTAL	GRAND TOTAL
	1	2	3	4	5	6	7	8	9	10		1	2	3	4	5	6	7	8	9	10		1	2	3	4	5	6	7	8	9	10		

Situated on the Warner Brothers Sunset Lot where the first talking picture in Hollywood was made.

"pinboys" to reset the pins and return the balls to the players. Pinsetters worked part-time and late hours and were generally unreliable ne'er-do-wells, creating a negative atmosphere particularly for women bowlers. By eliminating the pinboys, proprietors were able to keep the bowling centers open twenty-four hours a day, and encourage women and families to join in the fun. Large-scale air-conditioned bowling centers were being built across the country to meet the needs of families as they moved from the big cities to suburbia.

In the 1930s and 40s, large bowling houses fashioned their buildings in the streamlined Art Deco style in the same manner of large movie houses. In Hollywood, California, the Sunset Bowling Center was built on a Warner Brothers' lot. It was the largest in the world, boasting fifty-two lanes and covering an entire city block. In 1947, it was reported that Sunset clocked in 3,500 games in twenty-four hours, and Americans across the country were spending $200 million on bowling.

The Hollywood Recreation Center had a bar and lounge that featured nightly entertainment by the young Nat King Cole and the King Cole Trio. Hollywood's publicity machine published photos and stories of celebrities participating in studio teams or enjoying a night out at the lanes. Metro-Goldwyn-Mayer produced film shorts featuring all-star bowling champion trickster Andy Varipapa. National magazines featured whiskey and beer advertisements of well-dressed, middle-class men

44 LANES — IN A ROW WITHOUT A POST — 44 LANES

1301 KEOWEE ST.   McCOOK BOWL   DAYTON, OHIO

Playdium
2625 NORTH CLARK ST.
CHICAGO, ILLINOIS
SHOW PLACE of the BOWLING WORLD

Bowl Bar

WISCONSIN DELLS
WISCONSIN

and women enjoying leisure time in bowling alleys.

The California architectural firm, Powers, Daly, and DeRosa, designed the most prolific and emulated multiuse bowling centers that incorporated grandiose lobbies, extravagant landscaping, huge parking lots, and glitzy, eye-catching exteriors and signage. Community rooms, restaurants, banquet rooms, cocktail lounges, teen snack bars, daycare centers, beauty salons, and even a laundromat were integrated into these buildings to provide a social environment and a sense of community for a growing population.

Bowling centers, like motels, restaurants, and cocktail lounges, decorated their establishments with imaginative themes: faraway places, historical time periods, and fantasy.

Although bowling provided families affordable prices in a "country club" setting, adults were able to enjoy a night out in the bowling center's swanky cocktail lounges. The Bowl Bar in Wisconsin featured the world's largest champagne glass. The Pyramid Room at the Covina Bowl in California was inspired by Ancient Egypt's central motif of pyramids and triangles.

Early television jumped on the bowling bandwagon, further promoting the sport. Looking to fill in programming, bowling contests on TV were simple to produce, and billed as "Exciting! Suspenseful! Terrific!" One such TV series was *Championship Bowling*, featuring Joe Wilson, who whispered his narration so as not to distract the champions as they vied for cash prizes. Milton Berle's *Jackpot*

Bowling, produced in 1959, embraced and promoted the sport with celebrity interviews and a round rolled for charity. TV viewers could choose up to ten different bowling shows a week during that time period.

The Pinsetter Cocktail pays homage to the technology that brought bowling into the mid-twentieth century. Jason Snopkoski, bar director of Avanti Food and Beverage in Denver, Colorado, created this twist on a Julep, a popular midcentury drink.

 ## Pinsetter Cocktail

4–6 mint leaves
½ ounce honey syrup (mix 1 part honey to 1 part water, warm in a saucepan until dissolved and cool)
½ ounce Bénédictine

1 ounce rye whiskey
1 ounce cognac
Several dashes Angostura bitters
Mint sprig, for garnish

Muddle mint leaves, honey syrup, and Bénédictine in a large rocks glass. Fill glass two-thirds with crushed or cracked ice. Add rye and cognac. Stir, pressing the mint back to the bottom. Fill glass with ice and top with Angostura bitters. Garnish with a sprig of mint.

Offshore, the Territories, and Across the Border

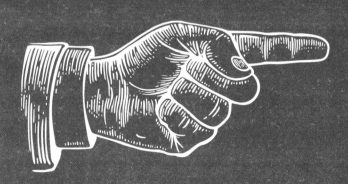

MOANA HOTEL, HONOLULU

4A-H789

Cooper's Ranch Punch

Victor Bergeron, restaurateur and mastermind of innumerable cocktail concoctions, wrote in his *Trader Vic's Book of Food and Drink* (1946), "Of all the liquors the world over, rum is really my meat—nectar of the gods, the drink of the ancients." Bergeron, the man behind the name Trader Vic, developed Polynesian-style restaurants and bars throughout the world from the 1940s to the 1960s, featuring his inventive potent and exotic libations.

Bergeron started in the restaurant business with a nickel-beer and dime-burger joint called Hinky Dinks in Oakland, California in 1934. Soon after, he reinvented the business to reflect a South Sea island vibe and served Cantonese-style meals, inspired by the decor and menu at Don the Beachcomber's tropical-themed restaurant. It was his fantastical drinks, a mélange of rums mixed with exotic fruit juices, that brought notoriety to his name and establishments.

In the early 1950s, Bergeron was commissioned by the Matson Steamship Line to create a Menehune-motif menu and bar list for its passenger ships and the Royal Hawaiian, Moana, and Surfrider Hotels in Oahu, Hawaii. The Menehunes were diminutive mythical Hawaiian people, who only came out at night to accomplish great feats. It was here that Bergeron introduced the Mai Tai and nine other cocktails of his own invention on the cruise ships and hotels. The Mai Tai became wildly popular; the other drinks quickly forgotten. Guests enjoyed the Menehunes menus as souvenirs.

Hula Girl, Hawaiian Islands

Bergeron was a master at marketing and promoting tourism in Hawaii. He was enchanted by Cooper's Ranch, a hotel and restaurant on the eighty-mile stretch around the island of Oahu. The ranch sat on a high bluff and had a spectacular view of the Pacific Ocean. It was noted for its fried chicken, coconut cream pie, and beautiful hibiscus gardens. Mrs. Cooper, the owner, decorated every inch of the inn with flowers. When Bette Davis visited the island, she sent her chauffeur every day to the Ranch to get one fresh white hibiscus flower. Bergeron enjoyed drinking the inn's signature cocktail, the Cooper's Ranch Punch. He noted that it was one of the few tropical drinks actually created in Hawaii.

Hawaiian Lei Vendors, Honolulu, T. H.

2B-H895

ROYAL HAWAIIAN HOTEL AT NIGHT, HONOLULU

COPYRIGHT P. P. HONOLULU

4A-H790

Hibiscus, Hawaiian Islands

 # Cooper's Ranch Punch

2 ounces Puerto Rican rum
2 ounces guava juice or guava jelly
2 ounces pineapple juice
1 ounce fresh lime juice
1 dash grenadine
Club soda or seltzer

Fill a 12-ounce glass with cracked ice. Add rum and the
rest of ingredients, except for the soda. Stir and fill rest of
the glass with soda or seltzer.

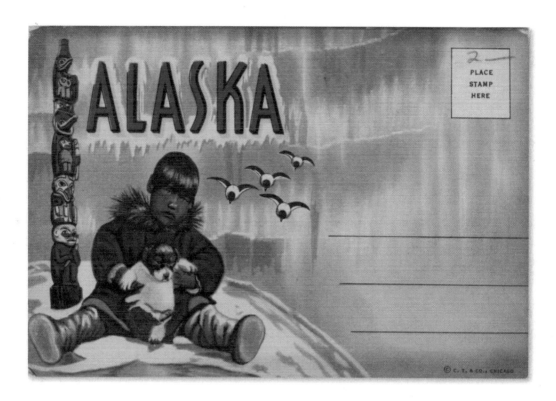

Alaska Cocktail

US Secretary of State William Seward arranged to purchase Alaska from Russia in 1867 and the criticized treaty became known as "Seward's Folly." Alaska proved its worth when gold was discovered and the first major gold rush in 1898 created an influx of prospectors seeking their fortune. By 1913, the gold strikes were dwindling, but Alaska's value as a territory rich in resources was established. Alaska officially became a state in 1959.

During the gold rush days, cities such as Skagway, Juneau, and Nome had ostentatious bars and saloons offering booze and entertainment to miners flush with gold in their pockets. The Alaskan natives, the Inuits, did not fare well with exposure to the "firewater" brought by the explorers. Men far outnumbered women, and social problems and crime appeared to increase as a result of excessive alcohol consumption. As a US territory, Alaska was subjected to the rules of Prohibition.

643:—FAMOUS ALASKA HUSKY

49038

RED DOG SALOON
"LIKE OLD TIMES"
JUNEAU, ALASKA

After repeal, limitations concerning alcohol remained in place. To this day, Alaska has some of the strictest policies regarding alcohol in the country.

Named for America's 49th state, the Alaska Cocktail was most likely created elsewhere and appears in a variety of early twentieth-century cocktail books including *The Savoy Cocktail Book* (1930). The exact origin of the Alaska Cocktail is unknown but documentation of the drink appears as early as 1914. The combination of gin, Yellow Chartreuse liqueur, and orange bitters create a pleasing golden-hued cocktail reminiscent of the Alaskan gold rush years. A departure from the simple shots of whisky that prospectors purchased with gold dust at local saloons, this sophisticated combination has a potency any explorer would appreciate.

Alaska Cocktail

2 ounces gin
1 ounce Yellow Chartreuse
1 dash orange bitters
Lemon peel, for garnish

Add the ingredients into a mixing glass with ice. Stir with a long-handled spoon and strain into a chilled cocktail glass. Garnish with a lemon peel.

Hotel Rivera Pacifico, Ensenada, Baja California, Mexico

"Where time is measured by day and night" Bougainvillaea Patio

Margarita

The Hotel Rivera del Pacifico in Ensenada, Mexico, opened in October 1930 with Xavier Cugat and His Orchestra presiding over the festivities. It was originally known as the Hotel Playa and built by a group of investors, most notably Jack Dempsey. The luxurious two million dollar complex was famous for its gambling hall and alcohol, especially during Prohibition. By 1938, the hotel closed due to the Depression and abolition of gambling in Mexico.

Ten years later, the hotel's owner, Jerome D. Utley, decided to bequeath the inactive hotel to a woman he was in love with named Marjorie King Plant, thirty years his junior. Marjorie, a noted beauty, began her career as a Ziegfeld showgirl in the 1920s and then acted in a number of B-movies in Hollywood. In 1939, she married Philip Plant, a millionaire playboy and big-game hunter. She was widowed two years later. When Mr. Utley offered Marjorie the hotel, she readily accepted.

MARJORIE KING

805 Hollywood Boulevard, Hollywood, California

7A-H3650

126—Daily Crowds on Avenida Revolucion, Tijuana, Mexico

0C-H958

As she traveled back and forth from California to Mexico negotiating the hotel's acquisition, she stopped in Tijuana and frequently patronized a small hotel and bar called the Rancho La Gloria. Its close proximity to California made it a popular hangout for the Hollywood set heading to the coastal towns in Mexico. Mickey Rooney, Vincent Price, and Walt Disney (a non-drinker) were regular guests at the bar. One day, Marjorie asked Danny Herrera, the owner and bartender, to make a drink with tequila. Herrera experimented with Cointreau and lemon juice. Marjorie was quite pleased, so he named the drink in her honor. Margarita is Spanish for Marjorie. Try Herrara's Margarita with lemon for a "softer" flavor than today's standard lime version.

👉 Margarita

3 ounces tequila
2 ounces Cointreau
1 ounce fresh lemon juice
Lemon slice, for garnish

Drench the rim of a glass in lemon juice and dip in salt. Add ingredients to a cocktail shaker filled with ice. Shake and strain into the salt-rimmed glass. Garnish with a lemon slice.

Mary Pickford Cocktail

It's not surprising that a sweet and tart drink was named after America's first sweetheart, Mary Pickford, who started her career as a silent movie actress and became the nation's first "star." Her thirty-year film career included acting, writing, and producing, as well as founding United Artists with her husband, Douglas Fairbanks, and Charlie Chaplin. Both Pickford and Fairbanks were part owners of the Grauman's Chinese Theatre in Hollywood. They were the first official celebrities to leave their imprints in the cement walk.

Beloved by all, Mary and Douglas were America's "it" couple. Weekend parties at the couple's twenty-two-room Beverly Hills mansion Pickfair were frequented by the likes of Chaplin, Valentino, F. Scott Fitzgerald, and Albert Einstein. When gossip columnist Louella Parsons announced the couple's impending

PISCINA PRIVADA DE AGUA SALADA, HOTEL NACIONAL DE CUBA

PRIVATE SALT-WATER POOL, HOTEL NACIONAL DE CUBA

Habana, Hotel Nacional

National Hotel

9A-H2089

divorce in 1933, millions of fans were dismayed. In 1936, Mary hosted a CBS radio program bursting with celebrity gossip called *Parties at Pickfair.* It proved to be unpopular during the Great Depression.

Mary went on to become the co-founder of the Society of Independent Motion Picture Producers in 1941, along with Charlie Chaplin, Orson Welles, Walt Disney, David O. Selznick, and Samuel Goldwyn. Pickford later played an important role as a philanthropist and was active in the film preservation movement.

There are two stories surrounding the creation of the Mary Pickford Cocktail. Basil Woon's breezy and somewhat contrived book, *When It's Cocktail Time in Cuba*, calls the Pickford drink "the aristocrat of cocktails." Woon gives Fred Kaufman, the bartender at the Hotel Nacional de Cuba, credit for creating the drink to commemorate Pickford's visit to Cuba in the 1920s. However, the actress had not been to Cuba since 1911,

850—Residence of Mary Pickford, Beverly Hills, California

JA-H1073

when she was working for the Independent Movie Picture Company of America. American-born bartender Eddie Woelke, from the Jockey Bar at the Sevilla-Biltmore in Havana, is also attributed in creating the tropical drink in Pickford's honor. The Mary Pickford Cocktail was a popular drink at Sloppy Joe's Bar, although it was served with a dash of absinthe. It is quite possible that Mary Pickford's celebrity status, not her phantom visit to Cuba, was the reason for this tasty cocktail's name.

Mary Pickford Cocktail

1½ ounces white rum
1½ ounces pineapple juice
1 teaspoon grenadine
1 dash Maraschino liqueur

Add all the ingredients to a cocktail shaker and fill with ice. Shake and strain into a chilled cocktail glass.

Daiquiri: E. Hemingway Special

In the 1940s, Cuba was considered to be the "gayest tourist playground" in the West Indies. Americans sailed to Cuba on cruise ships like the *S.S. Florida* and enjoyed romantic days at sea. Once on land, visitors swam at fashionable beaches, took photos at the Capitol, and toured sugar plantations. Famous nightclubs and bars such as the El Floridita, Sloppy Joe's, and La Bodeguita del Medio were packed with party-going travelers.

Demonstration bars in Havana enticed thirsty American visitors to try tall frosted daiquiri cocktails. The *Brooklyn Daily Eagle's* description of Havana's daiquiris was quite enticing. It stated "the icy particles, smoking with frost, chill the clear transparent rum and glorify it into a drink fit for the Spanish lords and ladies whose ghosts hover nearby." If you weren't in the mood for rum, friendly invitations to sample crème de menthe and blackberry brandy were in the offering. Aside from cigars and maracas, rum was the most popular souvenir. Americans leaving Cuba walked up the gangplank laden with five duty-free bottles for about one-third the cost in the States.

The bartender noted for popularizing the daiquiri cocktail was Constantino Ribalaigua Vert, known as the "Cocktail King" and proprietor of the El Floridita bar in Havana. Ernest Hemingway frequented El Floridita when he lived there starting in the 1930s. "El Constante," as Constantino was also known, a seasoned bartender who experimented with cocktails in order to increase sales, used an American-made ice chipper in his creations. In the bar's give-away recipe book, a variety of daiquiris are listed, including one concocted personally for Hemingway in which the sugar is removed and the rum doubled. Another drink, the "E. Hemingway Special," is named after the bar's patron and includes a dash of grapefruit juice.

S. S. Florida, passing thru channel at Miami, Florida, upon arrival from Havana, Cuba 504

HABANA, PLAYA DE MARIANAO

MARIANAO BATHING BEACH

1B-H605

Daiquiri:
E. Hemingway Special

2 ounces white rum
½ ounce Maraschino liqueur
¾ ounce fresh lime or lemon juice
½ ounce fresh grapefruit juice
Lime wheel, for garnish

Shake with cracked ice; strain into chilled cocktail glass.
Garnish with a lime wheel.

TEQUILA SUNRISE
Lime
Tequila
Creme de Cassis
Grenadine

Home of the
Jai Alai
GAMES

FRONTON PALACIO

JAI ALAI SPECIAL
Lime
Orange
Creme de Cacao
Bacardi Rum

Jai Alai Special

The Jai Alai Special was the signature drink from the Frontón Palacio in Tijuana, Mexico. It was considered to be a new taste sensation in the 1930s. An English-language publication at the time quoted, "Fix me up a Jai Alai! This is the kind of drink that you don't know what's in it, and after four drinks you don't care what's in it!"

Jai Alai is a competitive and dangerous ball sport played in a three-sided court. It originated in the Basque region in Spain and is considered the fastest sport in the world. During the 1930s, it was considered an exclusive sport and entertainment for the wealthy. It was important "to see and be seen at the fronton," the building that housed the sports arena. The frontons enticed spectators to dine, dance, and drink in its swanky restaurants and cocktail lounges. The Jai Alai Cafe at the Frontón Palacio was famous for its fine food, gracious service, and strolling troubadours.

JAI LAI CAFE
(hi li)
Columbus' Most Metropolitan Restaurant   589 North High Street

M-117—Crowd at Jai Alai Matches, Miami, Fla.

OB-H1354

German-born Eugene Hoffmann designed the Palacio in 1926, but it was not completed until 1947 due to downturns in the Mexican economy. The architecture reflected Jai Alai's Spanish origins in the Moorish tradition. The building's grandeur and fine aesthetic was distinctive and unparalleled in Tijuana. For fifty-one years, the Palacio's landmark building was a tourist attraction, seating 2,100 spectators for tournaments.

Jai Alai's popularity spread across Cuba, Mexico, the Philippines, and the United States in the early half of the twentieth century. The first fronton in America was built at the St. Louis World's Fair in 1904. Many more were built across the country over the next few decades. In 1938, the Hippodrome, the world's largest theater located in New York City, was converted to a fronton and billed as the newest entertainment on Broadway. Babe Ruth was a big fan of Jai Alai and was asked to manage the fronton at the Hippodrome, but this never came to pass.

The opening day party was quite an affair. Waitresses sported mantillas and ornate hair combs. An enormous bar was laden with alcohol and salami and goose liver sandwiches. Jai Alai players and patrons danced the shag to Slim Gaillard's new hit, "Flat Foot Floogie." Cocktail lounges and restaurants soon sprang up around the country with the Jai Alai moniker. The Jai Alai Lounge in Newport, Kentucky, touted this message on their postcard, "delicious drinks are made for the connoisseur, priced for the average person."

Jai Alai Special

1½ ounces light rum
1 ounce crème de cacao
Juice of 2 limes
1 ounce fresh orange juice

Pour rum, crème de cacao, and lime juice in a cocktail shaker with ice. Strain into glass and add orange juice.

"Jai Alai" (say Hi-Li) World's Fastest Sport, Biscayne Fronton, Miami, Florida

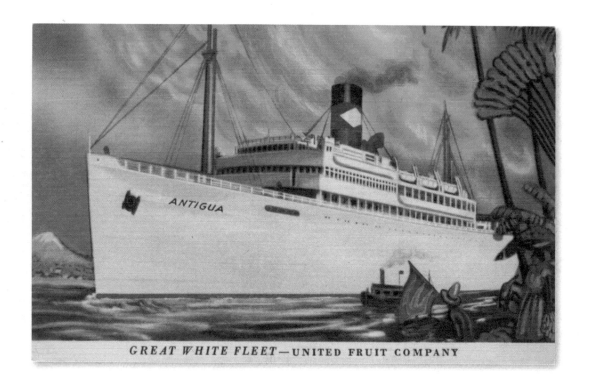

GREAT WHITE FLEET—UNITED FRUIT COMPANY

Three-Mile and Twelve-Mile Limit

During Prohibition, Americans boarded cruise ships to far-off places such as Europe, Hawaii, Mexico, Canada, and the Caribbean to enjoy cocktail time. Once the ocean liners passed the US coastline's territorial boundaries, alcoholic beverages were served. The evening's entertainment was as famous as the nightclubs in New York, striking "joy to the toes of those who love to dance!" Passenger line advertisements promised its wealthier travelers, "to sit in snug deckchairs, to idle, sip things, and watch the smart world go by."

Although Prohibition outlawed the sale, manufacture, and transport of intoxicating beverages, the three-mile, and later the twelve-mile, limit that was imposed around the United States did not actually prevent the import, export, and enjoyment of alcohol. It did help to boost cruise ship business, as well as illegal rum running from Canada, England, and the Caribbean.

Following the repeal of Prohibition, travelers continued to enjoy drinking, dining, and dancing on cruise ships. Ship directors and hostesses would entice travelers to dance to swing or jazz music, or enjoy a cabaret or folk dance performance. Shuffleboard, deck tennis, golf, swimming, horserace betting, pillow fights, and fancy dress balls were other interesting pursuits. These two aptly named cocktails thumb their nose at Prohibition, and are a tribute to glamorous times at sea. War correspondent and newspaper reporter Tommy Millard is said to have created the Twelve-Mile Limit recipe.

THE SS MARIPOSA, 632 FEET LONG; 79 FEET BREADTH; GROSS TONNAGE 19,000; SPEED 22½ KNOTS

☞ Three-Mile Limit

═══

2 ounces cognac
1 ounce white rum
1 teaspoon grenadine
1 dash fresh lemon juice

Shake all ingredients well with ice in a cocktail shaker and strain into a cocktail glass.

☞ Twelve-Mile Limit

═══

1 ounce white rum
½ ounce rye whiskey
½ ounce brandy
½ ounce grenadine
½ ounce fresh lemon juice
Lemon twist, for garnish

Shake all ingredients well with ice in a cocktail shaker and strain into a cocktail glass. Garnish with a lemon twist.

THE "BLUE SALON" - WORLD'S LARGEST FLOATING BALLROOM - STEAMER ADMIRAL

For Tots and Teetotalers

During America's post-war years, kids ruled. What could be better than going out with Grandma, Grandpa, Mom, Dad, aunts, and uncles for a special dinner at a fancy restaurant? There was often a build-up to the festive event; girls wore their finest patent leather shoes and boys their most colorful knitted vest. As menus were passed around the table, adults ordered Scotch on the rocks, gin and tonic, or the coveted Pink Lady Cocktail. With a special nod-of-the-head from one of the adults, the younger set were permitted to order from the kiddie corner of the menu and select a Shirley Temple or Roy Rogers concoction. Wow! What a thrill to have your very own "cocktail," just like the adults.

Child star Shirley Temple was such a sensation, a namesake drink was created just

Cowboy Riding a Jack Rabbit

for her pleasure. In the 1930s, Temple, the curly-haired, tap-dancing cutie, starred in numerous films such as *Bright Eyes* (1934), *The Littlest Rebel* (1935), and *Heidi* (1937). Temple's box office appeal was so great that by 1935, her weekly salary rose to $2,500 dollars per week. She was supplied with bodyguards, attendants, limousines, and her own charming bungalow at the studio. Reportedly, the Beverly Hills restaurant, Chasen's, created the nonalcoholic drink for her so she would have something to sip while dining with her adult companions.

Roy Rogers, the "King of the Cowboys," provided another dose of wholesomeness to the American scene. Rogers and his wife, Dale Evans, starred in the popular television series, *The Roy Rogers Show*, which aired from 1951 to 1957. The show featured Bullet, a dog, and Trigger, a trusty Palomino horse, who was capable of walking on his hind legs for fifty feet with Rogers on board. The combination of a cast dressed in elaborate western outfits, faithful animals, and six-shooters to catch "bad guys" was enough to make every child crave merchandise with the stars' image or endorsement. Rogers was said to be a teetotaler, providing the inspiration for an alcohol-free drink named in his honor.

713   BUNGALOW DRESSING ROOM OF SHIRLEY TEMPLE.

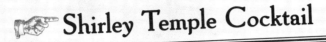 Shirley Temple Cocktail

1 dash grenadine
Ginger ale
Maraschino cherry, for garnish

Place grenadine in a tall glass and fill with ice,
pour ginger ale soda to top of the glass, and garnish
with a maraschino cherry.

 Roy Rogers Cocktail

1 dash grenadine
Cola soda
Maraschino cherry, for garnish

Place grenadine in a tall glass and fill with ice, pour cola soda
to the top of the glass, and garnish with a maraschino cherry.

Acknowledgments

It all started with vintage postcards, two enthusiastic collectors, and a cocktail. One afternoon, while pouring through our postcard collections, we came upon an idea. We noticed that many of our old postcards from America's post-Prohibition years were linked to period cocktails. It was the fun of sharing our collections and researching the past that led to the creation of this book.

During the early stages of our endeavor we were fortunate to meet Certified Wine and Spirits Specialist Douglass Miller. A generous mentor, Doug spent countless hours sharing his knowledge of cocktail history and expertise in mixology. We relished our meetings, which were instrumental in spurring our project forward.

Much of the joy we experienced in researching our book was from the fascinating people we encountered. Frank Caiafa, author of *The Waldorf Astoria Bar Book*, generously offered assistance researching and securing cocktail recipes. Frank, along with mixologists Jim Hewes, Lucinda Sterling, Douglass Miller, and Jason Snopkoski, read our feature stories and miraculously interpreted them into cocktail creations for our book.

It was a pleasure to meet Hotel New Yorker historian, Joseph Kinney. Joe's collection of hotel artifacts and his vast knowledge of the supper club entertainment that existed at the New Yorker provided a tangible taste of life in the post-Prohibition years. Professional ice skating historian, Roy Blakey, was kind enough to share some vignettes from his experience as a professional ice

DINE AND DANCE ON THE SPANISH VILLA

SOUTHERN HOTEL — BALTIMORE, MD.

6A-H485

TIP TOP TAP
ALLERTON HOTEL
CHICAGO, ILL.

HOTEL WEBSTER HALL COCKTAIL LOUNGE

5TH AVE. AT DITHRIDGE STREET — PITTSBURGH, PA.

5A-H1046

skater and his knowledge of the supper club "tank" shows that were once a popular night club entertainment.

We had the opportunity to connect to several libraries across the country. Nicole Semenchuk, Archives and Digital Collections Specialist at the Culinary Institute of America in Hyde Park, New York, was particularly helpful. A fan of vintage ephemera, Nicole graciously researched vintage menus and cocktail books for obscure recipes. We appreciate the assistance offered by staff members at the Julia L. Butterfield Memorial Library in Cold Spring, New York; the Howland Public Library in Beacon, New York; The Newberry, Chicago's Research Library in Chicago, Illinois; and the New York Public Library in New York, New York.

It was extremely helpful to have professional editor Robin Weisberg as a resource. Robin generously polished our work and helped prepare our proposal for presentation using her grammatical wizardry.

HOTEL BRADFORD CIRCUS ROOM BOSTON, MASS.

We experienced an exciting and memorable day when we met Michael Tizzano at The Countryman Press in New York City to discuss our book proposal. Michael believed in our work and made our book a reality. We appreciate the support of the team at Countryman, including Editorial Director Ann Treistman, as well as Devon Zahn, Jess Murphy, Anna Reich, Natalie Eilbert, and the many others who made this book possible.

Another great fortune was securing our astute literary agent, Mitchell S. Waters, from Curtis Brown, Ltd., in New York, NY. Mitchell patiently answered our many questions and helped us understand the inner workings of the publishing world.

We are grateful to our friends and colleagues at the Taconic Postcard Club in Yorktown Heights, New York, and The Metropolitan Postcard Club in New York City. Both clubs have provided informative programs cultivating our interest and knowledge in postcard collecting.

It is essential to recognize our family members who lent their ears to a tireless set of questions and ideas during the creative phase of this book. Thanks to Marisa Davis, Andrew Davis, Sarah Kuras, Evan Kuras, Felix Lara, and Ted Allen for your input on style, recipes, marketing, and social media. To Peter Lapis and Clifford Davis, our dear husbands, who provided encouragement, constructive guidance, and unwavering support through all aspects of the book's creation, we offer a hardy "Cheers!"

Index